string**CRAFT**

stringCRAFT

CREATE **35** FANTASTIC PROJECTS

by winding, looping, and stitching with string

LUCY HOPPING

CICO BOOKS
LONDON NEW YORK

Published in 2016 by CICO Books
An imprint of Ryland Peters & Small Ltd
20–21 Jockey's Fields   341 E 116th St
London WC1R 4BW   New York, NY 10029

www.rylandpeters.com

10 9 8 7 6 5 4 3 2 1

A CIP catalog record for this book is available from the Library of
Congress and the British Library.

ISBN: 978 1 78249 361 7

Printed in China

Editor: Marie Clayton
Designer: Isobel Gillan
Photographer: Jo Henderson
Illustrator: Louise Turpin
Technique illustrations and templates: Stephen Dew
Stylist: Jo Thornhill

In-house editor: Anna Galkina
Art director: Sally Powell
Head of production: Patricia Harrington
Publishing manager: Penny Craig
Publisher: Cindy Richards

Contents

Introduction

String craft is one of the most recent retro arts to be rediscovered, and updated for contemporary tastes. Forget the brown and orange swirly-patterned string crafts from the past; in this book random geometric shapes, ombré effects, and using the techniques in unusual ways bring string craft right up to date. As well as more traditional wall art, the 35 projects cover accessories, homewares, greeting cards, and more, to really push the limits of your imagination.

The first recorded use of string craft was by an English woman called Mary Everest Boole in the late 19th century. She used straight lines to create curved shapes, in the hope that it would help children understand the mathematical concept of the Bezier curve. But by the 1970s, filology—as geometric string craft can be known—was a huge craze. Threads wrapped around pins or nails, layered up to create intricate pictures and designs, graced many fashionable homes. Curved stitching uses the same concept—but instead of the threads being wrapped around pins, the lines are stitched into fabric or card.

Chapter 1, Display and Decorate, explores the ways that string craft can be used to create beautiful items for the home. Stunning wall-art pieces, made from driftwood or old pallets, update the old classics and make use of wood you may find on country walks or city explorations! Show off your stitching skills on stylish Stitched Canvas Placemats (see page 44), a Geometric Stitched Lampshade (see page 20), or a Funky Wastepaper Bin (see page 51).

In the second chapter, Accessories and Jewelry, we show you lots of cool ways to make your string craft into wearable items. The Day of the Dead Shopper (see page 69) is a particularly striking design, while the wooden Bird Brooches (see page 64) are perfect for everyday, pinned to a jacket lapel.

Artful Gifts, the final chapter, is jam-packed with smaller projects, perfect for beginners. The Yarn-covered Letters (see page 84) would make a wonderful present for a new baby, the colorful Stitched Notebooks (see page 82) will brighten up any day at work, and celebrate a special occasion by sending greetings with a Stitched Greeting Card (see page 94).

I hope these projects will whet your appetite for the possibilities of string craft. The skill levels of the projects are marked with one, two, or three stars, depending on complexity. Once you master the one star basics, try the two or three star makes, and after that you can begin developing your own designs and applying them to anything and everything that can be stitched, wrapped, or threaded!

Techniques

Running stitch

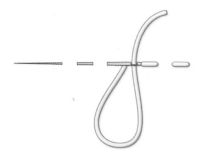

Secure the end of the thread with a few small stitches. Push the needle down through the fabric a stitch length along, then bring it back up through the fabric another stitch length along. Repeat to form a row of evenly sized and spaced stitches.

Backstitch

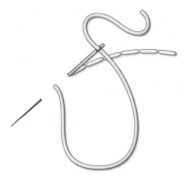

Start as if you were sewing running stitch. Sew one stitch and then bring the needle back up to start the second stitch. This time, instead of going forward, go back and push the needle down through the fabric at the end of your first stitch. Bring it out again a stitch length past where the thread emerges. Keep going to make an even line of stitches that touch one another with no gaps.

Straight stitch

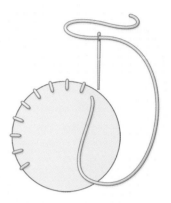

Work a series of single straight stitches, working around in a circle with the stitches radiating from the center as shown here, or with the stitches placed at random angles.

Satin stitch

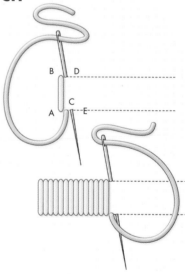

Bring the needle up at A, down at B, up at C right next to A, down at D next to B, and up at E, and so on, working all the stitches close together so that no fabric shows in between them.

Blanket stitch

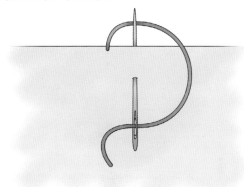

Bring the needle through at the edge of the fabric. Push the needle back through the fabric a short distance in from the edge and a stitch length along, and loop the thread under the needle. Pull the needle and thread through to make the first stitch.

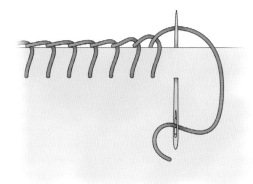

Make another stitch to the right of this and again loop the thread under the needle. Continue along the fabric, and finish with a few small stitches or a knot on the underside.

French knot

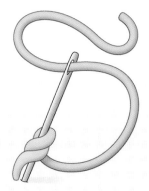

Knot the thread and bring the needle up from the back of the fabric to the front. Wrap the thread once or twice around the tip of the needle, then push the needle back in, right next to the place where it came up. As you push the needle in with one hand, hold the wrapped-around threads tightly against the fabric with the thumbnail of your other hand. Pull the needle all the way through. The wraps will form a knot on the surface of the fabric.

Adding a jump ring/clasp

To open a jump ring, hold a pair of pliers on each side of the join in the ring and twist the pliers slightly in opposite directions to open up a gap. This moves the ends away from each other without pulling them apart and distorting the shape of the ring.

To close the ring, repeat the twisting action in reverse to bring the two ends back together neatly. If you open and close jump rings as shown here they will stay perfectly round.

chapter one

DISPLAY and DECORATE

driftwood FEATHER

Create a stunning piece of wall art using a piece of driftwood as your base. Try searching riverbanks and lakesides as well as the coast for your wood— you'll be surprised at what gems you can find!

★ ★ ☆

You will need

• Tracing paper

• Pencil

• Driftwood

• Masking tape

• ½ in. (13 mm) panel pins

• Hammer

• Sewing thread in teal, pale green, cream, coral

• Scissors

1 Copy the template on page 112 and use masking tape to fix it to a suitable surface on the piece of driftwood. Hammer a panel pin into each marked point.

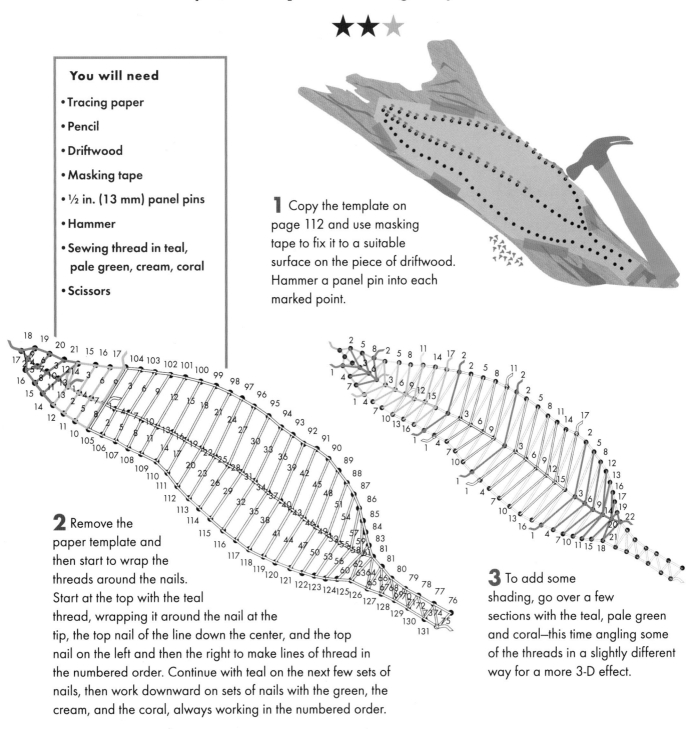

2 Remove the paper template and then start to wrap the threads around the nails. Start at the top with the teal thread, wrapping it around the nail at the tip, the top nail of the line down the center, and the top nail on the left and then the right to make lines of thread in the numbered order. Continue with teal on the next few sets of nails, then work downward on sets of nails with the green, the cream, and the coral, always working in the numbered order.

3 To add some shading, go over a few sections with the teal, pale green and coral—this time angling some of the threads in a slightly different way for a more 3-D effect.

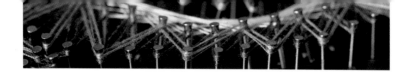

string art OWL

Twit twoo! Make this funky owl picture by wrapping thread between nails. Let your imagination and creativity go wild by layering threads, and combining freeform wrapping with neater, more precise sections.

★ ★ ★

You will need

- 12 x 12 in. (30 x 30 cm) piece of wood, ¼ in. (6 mm) thick
- Matt black spray paint
- ½ in. (13 mm) panel pins
- Hammer
- Masking tape
- Sewing thread in blue, light blue, light green, yellow, magenta, pale pink, orange, pale orange, peach, teal
- Scissors

1 Spray the piece of wood black and allow to dry.

2 Tape the template on page 112 onto the wood using the masking tape, then hammer a panel pin into each dot.

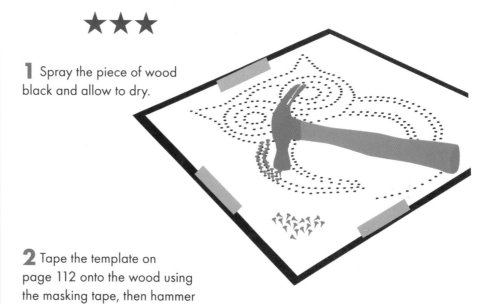

3 Gently remove the paper template. Start with the eyes: tie the blue thread to one of the inner circle nails and wrap around the nails in the order shown.

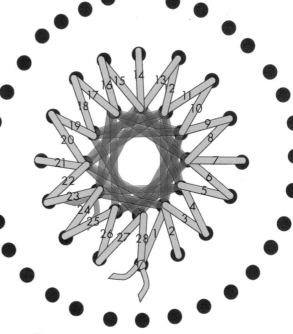

4 Then take the light blue and wrap around the nails in the order shown.

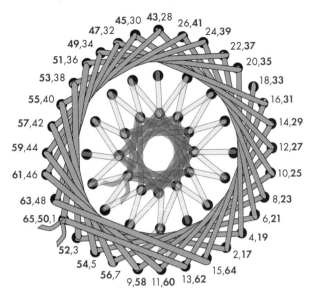

Numbers around the eye diagram (step 5):
45,30 43,28 26,41 24,39
47,32   22,37
49,34   20,35
51,36   18,33
53,38   16,31
55,40   14,29
57,42   12,27
59,44   10,25
61,46   8,23
63,48   6,21
65,50,1   4,19
52,3   2,17
54,5   15,64
56,7 9,58 11,60 13,62

5 To complete the eyes, take the light green thread and wrap around the nails in the order shown.

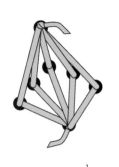

6 For the beak, attach the yellow thread to a beak nail and wrap as shown.

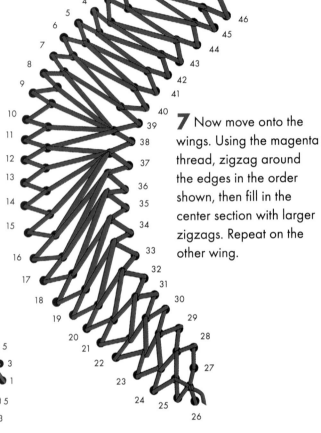

Numbers along the wing diagram (step 7):
1, 2, 3, 4, 5, 6, 7, 8, 9, 10, 11, 12, 13, 14, 15, 16, 17, 18, 19, 20, 21, 22, 23, 24, 25, 26, 27, 28, 29, 30, 31, 32, 33, 34, 35, 36, 37, 38, 39, 40, 41, 42, 43, 44, 45, 46, 47

7 Now move onto the wings. Using the magenta thread, zigzag around the edges in the order shown, then fill in the center section with larger zigzags. Repeat on the other wing.

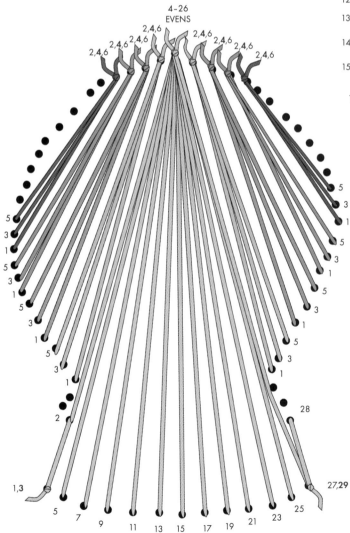

4–26
EVENS

2,4,6 2,4,6 2,4,6 2,4,6 2,4,6 2,4,6 2,4,6

Left side: 5, 3, 1, 5, 3, 1, 5, 3, 1, 5, 3, 1, 2, 1,3
Bottom: 5, 7, 9, 11, 13, 15, 17, 19, 21, 23, 25
Right side: 5, 3, 1, 5, 3, 1, 5, 3, 1, 5, 3, 1, 28, 27,29

8 Wrap threads as shown vertically to create the chest and tail, using the magenta, pale pink, orange, pale orange, and peach threads in order, from the outside inward, to create the shaded effect.

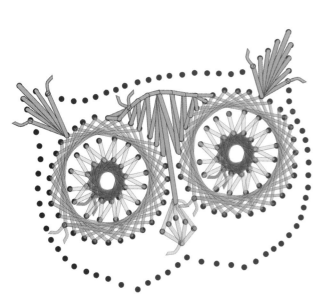

10 Finally, add a second layer of vertical peach, pale orange, and orange threads across the center of the chest and tail as in step 8.

9 Then add a layer of horizontal teal threads over the top of the chest section.

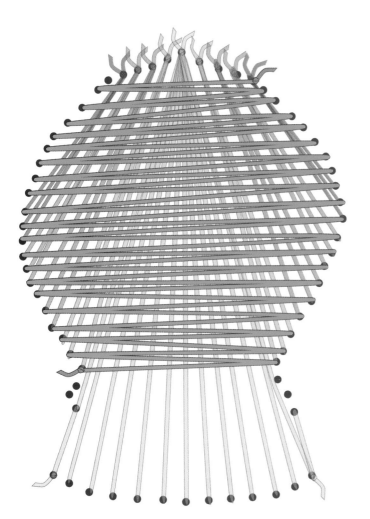

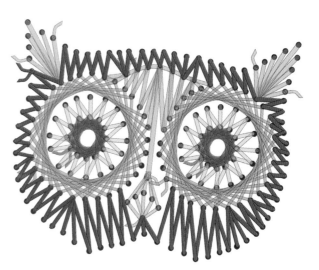

11 Now complete the face. Add layers of pink and pale pink thread in a random order—I added pale orange on the forehead and ears, and zigzags of orange and pale pink around the face.

geometric stitched LAMPSHADE

Inject some color into a plain white lampshade by stitching this cool geometric design into it. Choose shades that match your décor or add a pop of color by following this one.

★★☆

You will need

- Plain white lampshade and stand
- Ruler
- Pencil
- Cotton thread in turquoise, bright green, dusky pink, purple, acid yellow
- Sharp needle
- Scissors

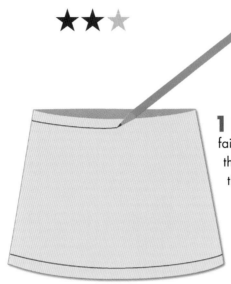

1 Using the pencil and ruler, draw faint lines ³⁄₈ in. (1 cm) down from the top and up from the bottom of the lampshade.

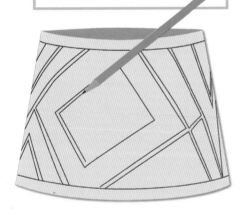

2 Using the template on page 113, lightly draw the design onto the lampshade. The size of the stripes will depend on the size of your lampshade, but mine are between ¾ in. (2 cm) and 1¼ in. (3 cm) wide with a ¼-in. (5-mm) gap between each one.

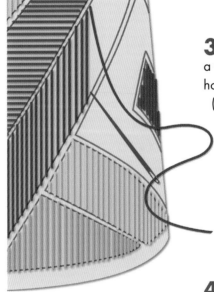

3 Stitch each section with a variety of vertical and horizontal spaced satin stitches (see page 8). Each stitch is the width of the section being filled and spaced approximately ¹⁄₁₆ in. (2 mm) away from the next.

4 Thread all loose ends in at the back and trim to finish.

button NOTICE BOARD

Update a dull notice board with some pretty floral fabric, and add strings to hold your papers in place. Decorate your thumbtacks with buttons and add them where the strings cross for a shabby chic effect.

★ ★ ★

You will need

- **16 x 12 in. (40 x 30 cm) notice board**
- **20 x 16 in. (50 x 40 cm) piece of gray floral fabric**
- **Glue gun and staple gun**
- **4 m of gold cord**
- **Scissors**
- **Approx. 10 thumbtacks**
- **Approx. 10 pink shell buttons**

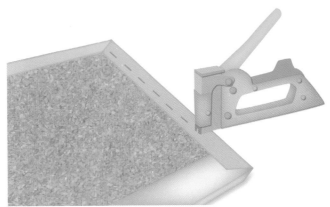

1 Place the fabric right side out on the front of the notice board and pull the edges round to the back so it's taut. Attach the fabric to the back of the board frame using a glue gun or staple gun.

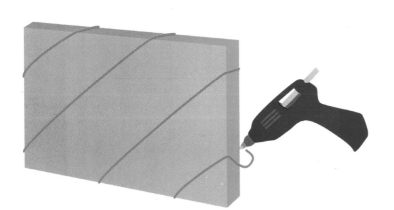

2 Lay the gold cord in diagonal lines across the board to form a grid, cutting the cord long so the ends will go over onto the back. Stick the ends in place on the back of the board frame and trim.

3 Push a thumbtack through the cords at each point where they cross. Stick a button to the top of each thumbtack.

embroidered STORAGE BASKETS

Brighten up your desk space with these wicker storage baskets, which have been decorated with a contemporary embroidery design.

★ ★ ★

You will need

- Wicker storage drawers
- Pencil and ruler
- Stranded floss in jade, orange, lilac, rust, purple, light gray
- Large needle
- Scissors

1 Start by drawing a grid onto one side of your wicker storage baskets. Here I've drawn a grid that will give the illusion of 3-D stacking cubes.

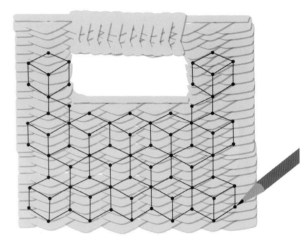

2 Thread the needle with your outline color floss, and sew large straight stitches (see page 8) all around the outlines of the grid.

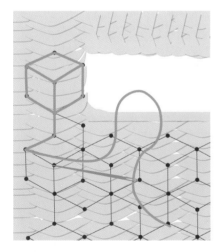

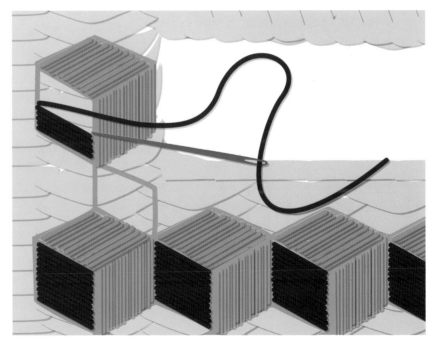

3 Now fill in the sides of the cubes using satin stitch (see page 8), choosing a dark color for the same side all along the row, then medium and light colors on the other two sides to create the 3-D effect.

yarn BOWL

Your friends and family will be "bowled" over by this little yarn bowl.
It is made from a simple handmade cord, created by joining yarn strands with a
machine zigzag stitch, which is then coiled and sewn together by hand.

You will need

- Cotton Aran yarn in mustard, teal, green, burnt orange, pinky-red
- Scissors
- Sewing machine
- Coordinating sewing thread
- Needle

1 Take three pieces of yarn, each a different color and each a slightly different length: 20 in. (50 cm), 30 in. (75 cm), 40 in. (100 cm). Align one end of each and start sewing the lengths together using zigzag stitch on the sewing machine.

2 As each color of yarn runs out, replace it with another color to create an ever-changing colored cord. Keep making the cord until it is about 22 yd. (20 m) long.

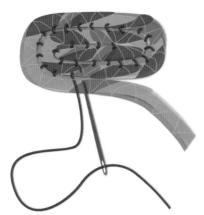

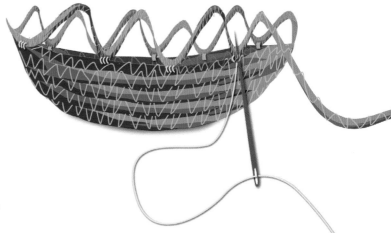

3 Now start making the bowl. Neaten one end of the cord by trimming and then fold the end over on itself by ⅝ in. (1.5 cm). Stitch in place with a few tiny hand stitches. Then begin coiling the cord, stitching it around this center section until the base is as large as you require.

4 To build up the sides, begin coiling the cord on top of the last round of the base, stitching in place as you go.

5 For the wave detail, create loops with the cord all round the bowl and stitch in place with a couple of stitches between each wave.

6 Continue working rows of cord and wave details until the bowl is the desired size and shape.

mandala DECORATION

Update the "Ojos de Dios" decorations you made at summer camp with this more intricate 8-sided, doubled-layered version. Then sew back into the weaving to create a really beautiful and detailed effect.

★ ★ ★

You will need

- Four 10½ in. (27 cm) wooden skewers
- Hacksaw
- Craft knife
- Ruler
- Pencil
- Cotton yarn in rust, peach, teal, mustard, pale blue
- Scissors
- Wool needle

1 Make a small ¼ x ¹⁄₁₆ in. (5 x 2 mm) notch in the center of each skewer, using the hacksaw to cut down and then a craft knife to gouge out the wood.

2 Interlock the notches to join two of the sticks into a cross. Wind the rust yarn around the join a couple of times to hold it in place.

3 Continuing with the rust yarn, and working in a counterclockwise direction, take it under the right stick, then over, round under, and up over the next stick to the left. Then move on to repeat the winding sequence on the next stick to the left.

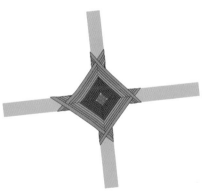

4 Work six rounds of the rust in this way, then two rounds of peach and three rounds of teal.

5 Take the second pair of sticks and repeat steps 1–4, but work eight rounds of teal at the end instead of three.

Tip

When you are working the rounds, you will need to weave the yarn under previous rounds in some cases to keep the pattern symmetrical and correct.

6 Place the smaller square of threads diagonally on top of the larger one and hold in place using two rows of mustard yarn on the top sticks and two rows of rust on the bottom. Work these rows diagonally right across the back so they hold the two squares together, and form dagger shapes on the sticks.

7 Continue working rounds, winding around one set of sticks and weaving under the other set between each round: wind four rounds of pale blue on the top sticks only (going under the bottom sticks); wind two rounds of teal on the bottom sticks only (going under the top sticks and the teal threads); wind four rounds of mustard on the top sticks (going under the bottom sticks); wind seven rounds of peach on the bottom sticks (going under the top sticks and under the mustard threads); wind eight rounds of teal on the top sticks (going under the bottom sticks); wind three rounds of pale blue on the bottom sticks (going under the top sticks and under the teal threads); wind three rounds of pale blue on the top sticks (going under the bottom sticks).

8 Now work ten rows of rust on the bottom sticks and ten rows of rust on the top sticks, but work the rows diagonally across the back to create dagger shapes on the sticks, as in step 6.

9 Then using the rounds technique as in steps 3, 4, 5, and 7, wrap eight rounds of peach on the bottom sticks (going under the top sticks), five rounds of mustard on the top sticks (going over the peach threads and under the bottom sticks), two rounds of teal on the bottom sticks (going under the top sticks and under the mustard threads), and two rounds of teal on the top sticks (going under the bottom sticks and under the teal and peach threads).

10 Next work six rows in mustard yarn on the bottom sticks only, working diagonally across the back to create dagger shapes on the sticks, as in steps 6 and 8.

11 To finish off, go round all the sticks in a counterclockwise direction with 16 rounds of pale blue, three rounds of rust and five rounds of mustard.

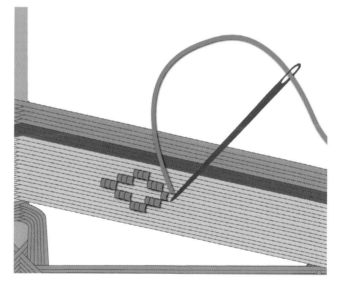

12 Using teal yarn, stitch a decorative design in straight stitches (see page 8) into the pale blue sections to finish the mandala.

air plant TERRARIUMS

Even the least green-thumbed gardener can hope to keep these air plants alive! Display them creatively on stringed backgrounds.

You will need

- 3 wooden placemats or pieces of wood a similar size
- Pencil
- Ruler
- Drill with ⅙-in. (2-mm) drill bit
- 3.5 mm screws
- Screwdriver
- Beading thread or similar cord in orange, mustard, green
- Scissors
- Terrarium plants
- Glue gun
- Moss

Triangle design

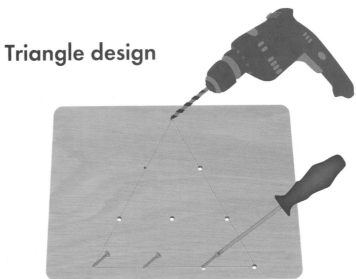

1 Draw an equilateral triangle on the back of the wooden base and divide each side into three equal lengths. Find the center point between the second pair of holes up from the base line, and mark this. Drill a hole at each point and add a screw to each.

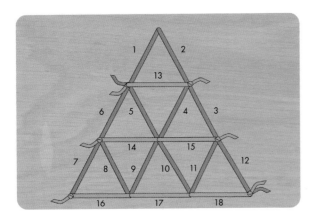

2 Take the orange cord, tie it to the top screw, and work around the other screws in the order shown from 1 to 12. You will have to wrap around most of the screws one-and-a-half times to get to the right position to wrap the next two screws, except on 3 and 7, where you wrap round twice. Tie and trim to the last screw. Now take the mustard thread and wrap sequence 13, then 14 to 15, then 16 to 18, tying off at the end of each sequence. Number 13 will need to be wrapped around twice, but the others are one-and-a-half times.

3 Use the glue gun to stick the roots of a plant in the gaps of the string as you wish. Use the moss to hide the roots and glue.

Rectangle design

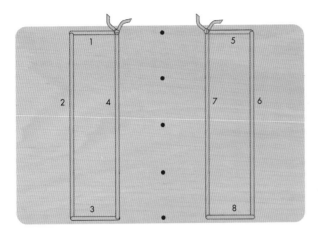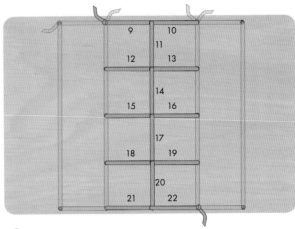

1 Follow the illustration to add the screws at key points. Follow the order of the wrapping, first using the mustard thread for sequences 1 to 4 and 5 to 8.

2 Then wrap the green thread for sequence 9 to 22. Numbers 9, 11, 14, 17, 20, and 22 are all wrapped one-and-a-half times; everything else is wrapped twice.

3 Add plants as you wish. I had two long plants, so I added them on either side.

Circular design

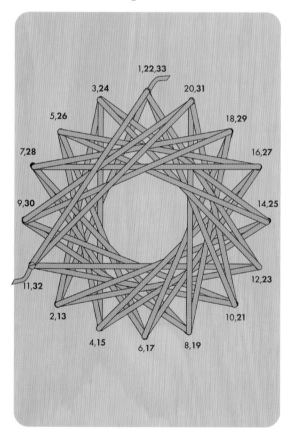

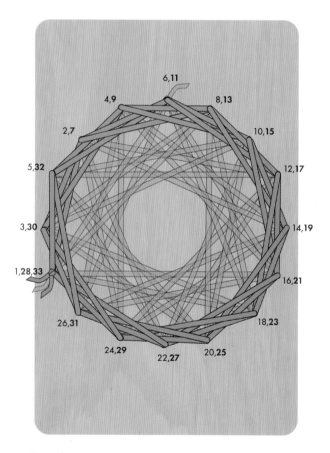

1 Add 16 screws equally placed around a circle. Wrap the green string in the order shown, from 1 to 32.

2 Now take the orange thread and wrap in the order shown, from 1 to 33.

3 Add the plant and moss to the center as before.

string DREAMCATCHER

Dreamcatchers make great wall decorations—and this one has a heart in its center, as well as pompom and felt decorations.

★★☆

You will need

- Wire
- Embroidery hoop
- String
- Scissors
- Fabric paint in red, lilac, turquoise
- Paintbrush
- Wool in turquoise, pink, orange, lilac
- Felt in olive green, magenta, turquoise, pale green
- Needle
- Stranded floss in olive green, magenta, turquoise, pale green
- Turquoise cotton cord
- Wooden beads in lime green, turquoise, pink

1 Make a heart shape from the wire and place it in the center of the embroidery hoop. Wind around with the string to attach the two shapes together.

2 Paint the strings with fabric paint, starting with red in the center, then lilac, and turquoise on the outside. Allow to dry.

3 Make a pompom by wrapping the turquoise wool around three fingers until you have a good hank. Wrap the ends around the center and tie a tight knot.

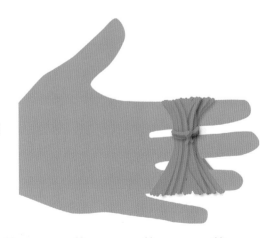

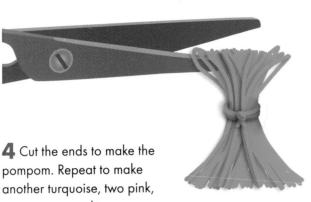

4 Cut the ends to make the pompom. Repeat to make another turquoise, two pink, two orange, and two lilac pompoms.

5 Now make the felt hearts. Cut two of each size in the colors shown on the templates on page 113. Sew together around the edge using blanket stitch (see page 11) in a contrasting thread.

6 Cut three lengths of cord, each 40 in. (100 cm) long and thread one end of each through the bottom of the strings on the embroidery hoop, spacing them apart evenly. Thread the hearts, pompoms, and beads onto the string in a random order using the photograph as a guide.

7 Finally thread a 12 in. (30 cm) cord through the strings at the top of the hoop to hang the dreamcatcher.

flowers in a JAR

Mason jars are very trendy—and with this project your jar will never get smashed, the flowers will never wilt, and you can hang it on a wall!

You will need

- Tracing paper
- Pencil
- 3 pieces of wood, each approx. 7¼ x 3½ in. (18 x 9 cm)
- Approx. 6 x 10 in. (15 x 25 cm) piece of wooden board
- 130 nails, size ⅝ in. (15 mm)
- Hammer
- Tape
- Lilac cotton thread
- Faux flowers
- Glue gun (optional)

1 Trace the template on page 114 onto the tracing paper. Arrange the wooden pieces face down, place the board on top, and nail them together, making sure these nails don't come through onto the front. Turn over so the pieced wood side is facing upward.

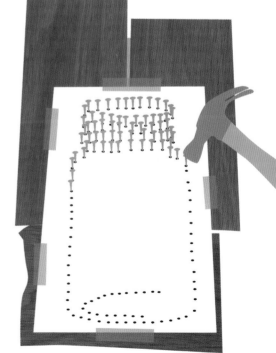

2 Tape the tracing paper to the pieced wood. Hammer a nail partly into the wood at each dot of the template. Remove the tracing paper from the wood.

3 Take a length of lilac thread and tie one end to one of the nails at the end of a line. Wrap in a figure of eight and then right around both nails. Go on to the next nail and wrap this in a figure of eight with the previous nail, then go right around these two nails.

4 Repeat the wrapping along all the nails to create a line of the drawing. Tie off and trim at the end of the line. Repeat steps 3 and 4 to create all the lines of the jar.

5 Thread the flowers through the top of the "jar," then glue in place with a glue gun, if necessary.

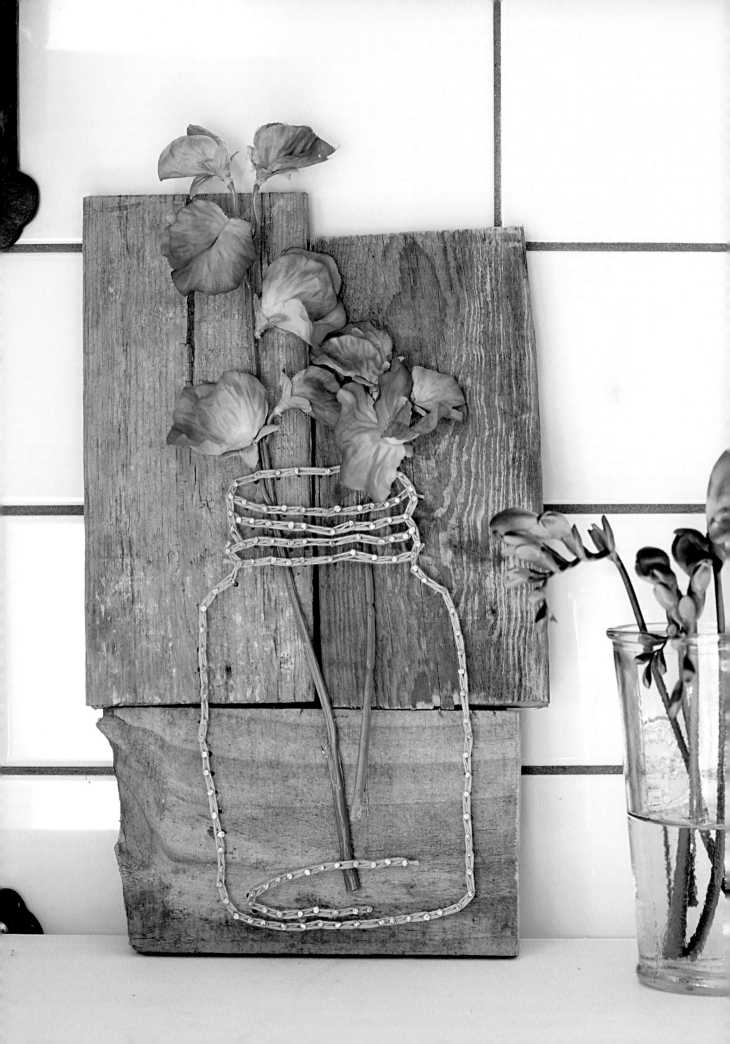

STAG'S HEAD picture

Create a sectioned wooden wall hanging using an old wooden pallet, nails, and some cotton thread. The effect when hung together is staggering!

★★☆

You will need

- Tracing paper
- Pencil
- Scissors
- Wooden storage pallet or 3 x ¾ in. (7.5 x 2 cm) wooden planks
- Ruler
- Saw
- Sandpaper
- Tape
- 520 nails, size 5/8 in. (15 mm)
- Hammer
- Burgundy cotton thread
- 16 picture hanging hooks

1 Trace the template on page 115 onto the tracing paper, making sure you include the grid. Cut the template into the sixteen separate squares.

2 Cut the wood into sixteen 3-in. (7.5-cm) squares. Sand the pieces to remove any splinters. Tape a square of the paper template to each piece of wood.

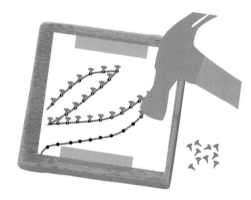

3 Hammer a nail into the wood at each dot of the template.

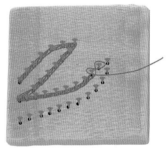

4 Remove the tracing paper from the wood. Cut a length of burgundy cotton thread and tie the end to one of the nails at the end of a line of the design. Wrap in a figure of eight and then right around both nails. Go on to the next nail and wrap this in a figure of eight with the previous nail, then go right around these two nails.

5 Repeat the wrapping along all the nails to create a line of the drawing. Tie off and trim at the end of the line.

6 Repeat on all the pieces to "draw" your picture. Nail a hanging hook on the back of each wooden piece to complete, then hang the pieces together in order.

stitched canvas PLACEMATS

These stylish mid-century-inspired placemats will look wonderful at any dinner party, or just for day-to-day living. Made from plastic canvas, they really are an updated retro craft.

You will need

- 2 pieces of plastic canvas, each approx. 13 x 9¼ in. (32.5 x 23.5 cm)
- 2 pieces of plastic canvas, each approx. 3¾ in. (9.5 cm) square
- Pencil
- Ruler
- Cotton yarn in pink, cream, teal, gray, aqua, mustard
- Yarn needle
- Scissors

1 Count the holes across the length and width of each piece of canvas—the placemats should each be 85 x 61 holes. The two drinks mats should each be 25 x 25 holes.

2 For the pink/cream/teal placemat, mark horizontally along the 13th line of holes down from the top. Repeat on every 12th line of holes after this. Mark vertically along the 13th line of holes from the left edge. Repeat on every 12th line of holes after this. Each square of this grid will take one repeat of the stitched motif. Using pink yarn, make five long diagonal stitches in the top left section of the first square, as shown.

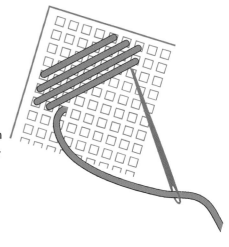

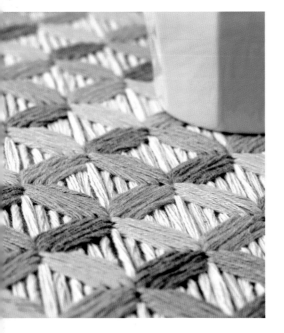

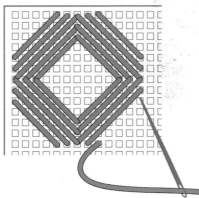

3 Repeat the sequence of stitches in the other three corners of the square, with the stitches that butt up to each other sharing the same hole.

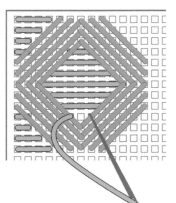

4 Start to fill in the gaps with cream horizontal stitches.

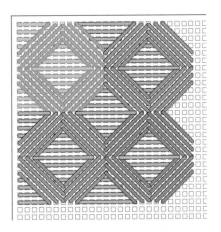

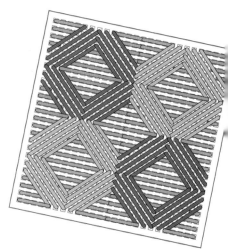

5 Use teal yarn to work the next square motif in the same way, alternating teal and pink motifs across the mat in a checkerboard design and filling in the gaps between the shapes with cream horizontal stitches. Adjoining motifs share the lines of stitching holes marked in step 2.

6 For the matching drinks mat, work in the same way but use gray and aqua threads, with infill stitches in mustard.

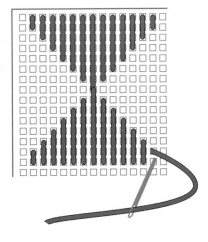

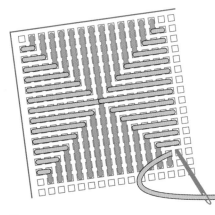

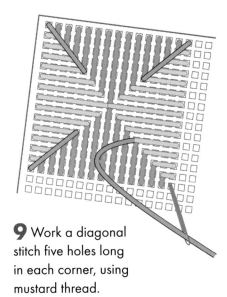

7 For the gray/aqua/mustard placemat, mark horizontally along the 15th line of holes down from the top. Repeat on every 14th line of holes after this—you'll have an extra four rows of holes along the bottom edge after the last line. Mark vertically along the 15th line of holes from the left edge. Repeat on every 14th line of holes after this. Each square of this grid will take one repeat of the stitching pattern. Using gray yarn, make 13 stitches to form a triangle in the top half of the first square and a mirrored triangle in the bottom half, as shown.

8 Using aqua, repeat the triangles of stitching on each side of the square, with the stitches that butt up to each other sharing the same hole.

9 Work a diagonal stitch five holes long in each corner, using mustard thread.

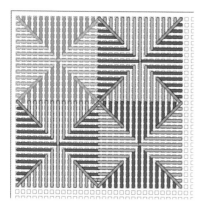

10 Repeat the design across the mat, alternating the gray and aqua as shown. Adjoining motifs share the lines of stitching holes marked in step 7. For the extra four lines of holes at one long edge, fill with part of the motif, keeping the design as set.

11 To make the matching coaster, follow the pattern but use pink, teal, and cream thread.

OMBRE canvases

Create a quartet of canvases with nails and colored threads. Each canvas has one more layer of thread than the previous, so a gorgeous gradated shading effect is created.

★ ★ ★

You will need

- 4 canvases, each 8 x 8 in. (20 x 20 cm)
- Pencil and ruler
- Hammer
- 576 panel pins
- Sewing thread in turquoise, purple, green
- Scissors

1 Coming in $^3/_8$ in. (1 cm) from the edge of the canvas, mark dots evenly along each edge so there are 37 marks along each side. Hammer a panel pin into each mark. Repeat on all four canvases.

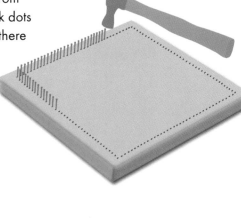

2 Using the illustration as a guide, take the turquoise thread and tie it to the nail one down from the top left corner, on the left side. Go up to the nail one to the right from the top left corner, on the top edge. Continue in this way, wrapping diagonally between the left side and the top edge until you reach the halfway point, then tie off the turquoise thread. Tie the purple thread to the last turquoise nail and then wrap the next set of 10 nails diagonally using purple. Now tie the green thread to the last purple nail and work the green threading sequence to the last pair of nails in the bottom right corner, then tie off. Trim the ends.

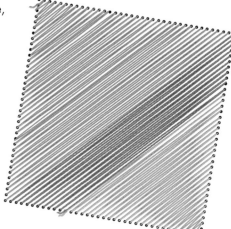

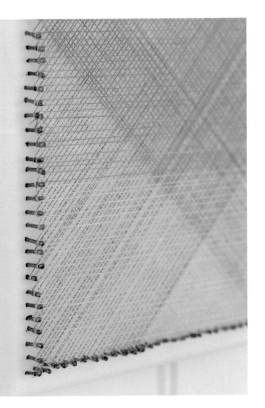

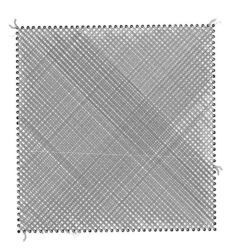

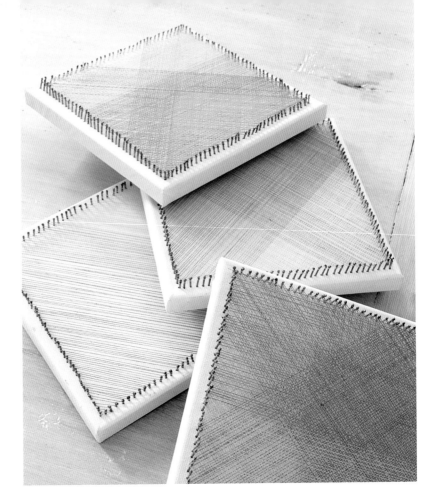

3 On the next canvas, repeat step 2. Then work the threading sequence at the opposite angle, so the turquoise thread begins bottom left and you work the threading sequence, changing colors as before, finishing with green at the top right corner.

4 On the next canvas repeat steps 2 and 3. Then work vertical lines, starting with the turquoise thread tied onto the nail one to the right from the bottom left corner on the bottom edge, and working up to the corresponding nail on the top edge. Go down to the next nail to the right on the bottom edge and then straight up, and so on, until you've wrapped 16 nails across the top, then tie off the turquoise thread on the 17th nail at the bottom. Tie the purple thread to the same nail and wrap this vertically for 5 nails, tying off on the 6th nail at the bottom. Now tie the green thread to this same nail and work the green threading sequence to the end. Tie off and trim the ends.

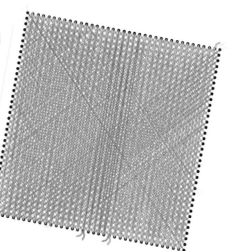

5 On the final canvas, repeat steps 2 to 4. Then work the threading sequence horizontally, so the turquoise thread begins bottom left and you work the threading sequence, changing colors as before, finishing with green at the top right corner.

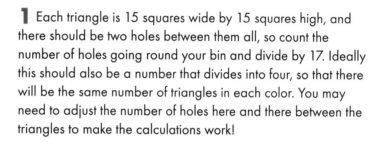

funky WASTEPAPER BIN

Upcycle a wire bin with two borders of stitched neon triangles. Stylish and funky, this would also be a great receptacle to store your wrapping papers and craft materials.

You will need

- Wire wastepaper bin
- Yarn in neon green, turquoise, cream, neon pink
- Yarn needle
- Scissors

1 Each triangle is 15 squares wide by 15 squares high, and there should be two holes between them all, so count the number of holes going round your bin and divide by 17. Ideally this should also be a number that divides into four, so that there will be the same number of triangles in each color. You may need to adjust the number of holes here and there between the triangles to make the calculations work!

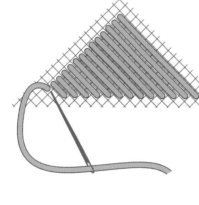

2 Cut a piece of neon green yarn and double up to thread it onto the needle. Starting three holes from the top edge of the bin, work a diagonal stitch that is 15 holes long. Make another stitch next to it 14 holes long and so on, until you have 14 stitches, with the last stitch being made between two adjoining holes.

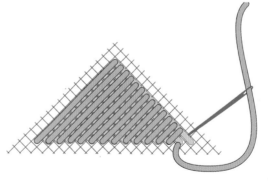

3 Then work 14 diagonal stitches going in the other direction over the top of the first set, beginning the first stitch in the hole immediately after the last stitch of the first triangle.

Tip

You will probably need to rework your calculations for the bottom of the bin because it is a smaller circumference than at the top, so there will be fewer holes around.

4 Change to turquoise yarn. Starting two holes (or according to your calculations in step 1, if this means you need more or fewer holes between each triangle) to the left of the first triangle, repeat the stitching in steps 2 and 3. Continue alternating green and turquoise triangles all around the bin.

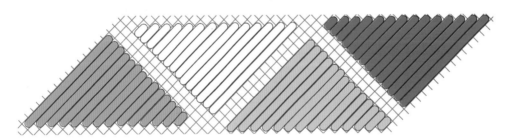

5 Now change to cream and pink yarn and work the triangles upside down in the spaces between the green and turquoise ones. They should be two squares up from the first set, again depending on your calculations in step 1.

6 Repeat the triangles, beginning three holes up from the bottom of the bin to create the bottom border.

rope MIRROR

Ahoy there! Make a nautical-style mirror using rope and some florist's wire. This would look great in a bathroom or above a mantelpiece.

★ ★ ☆

You will need

- 11 yd. (10 m) thin cream cord
- 5½ yd. (5 m) thick florist's wire
- Glue gun
- 12-in. (30-cm) diameter mirror
- 11-in. (27.5-cm) diameter felt circle

1 Wrap the cord around the length of wire, using the glue gun to stick it in place at intervals.

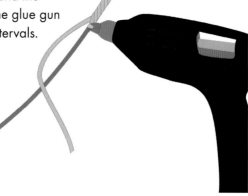

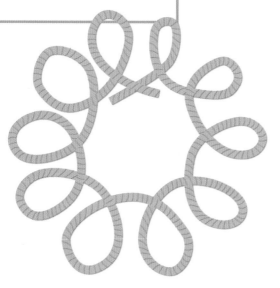

2 Once it's covered, loop the wire into hoops and shape it into a circle, slightly smaller than the circumference of the mirror. Twist the ends together to secure.

3 Glue the rope to the back of the mirror and cover with the felt circle.

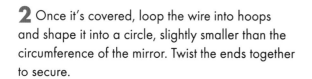

yarn-wrapped STOOL

Add some personality to a simple wooden stool by wrapping stripes of colorful wool around its legs! Whether for a kid's bedroom or workspace, this really is a great use for wool scraps.

You will need
• Double-stick tape
• Scissors
• Wooden flat-pack stool
• Yarn in red, turquoise, green, coral, cream, gray
• Yarn needle

1 Apply strips of double-stick tape to all four sides of one leg.

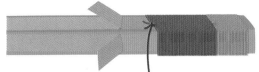

2 Peel away a small length of the backing on each strip of tape and tie a piece of yarn to the leg.

3 Begin to wrap the yarn around the leg, peeling the tape backing off farther as required. Change colors when you feel it's necessary, by tying the next color to the previous one and covering the loose ends with the wrapping. It's nice to combine thicker and thinner stripes.

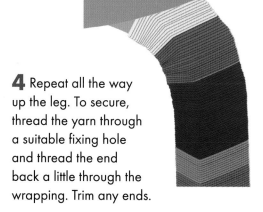

4 Repeat all the way up the leg. To secure, thread the yarn through a suitable fixing hole and thread the end back a little through the wrapping. Trim any ends.

5 Repeat on all legs, then assemble the stool according to the manufacturer's instructions.

Tip

This project is worked more easily if the stool has not been assembled.

chapter two

ACCESSORIES
and JEWELRY

embroidered BUTTONS

Jazz up a boring jacket or sweater with your own homemade buttons! Formed from air-dry clay and then painted and stitched, these will really brighten up your knits and more.

★ ★ ★

You will need

- Air-dry clay
- Rolling pin
- Sharp knife or tiny cookie cutter
- Toothpics
- Acrylic paint
- Paintbrush
- Stranded floss
- Needle

1 Take a piece of air-dry clay and roll out to a thickness of about ⅛ in. (4 mm). Cut out pieces to the size and shape you want your buttons to be. Here I have made a variety of squares, circles, and flowers.

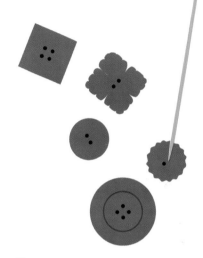

2 Using a toothpick make two or four holes all the way through the center of each button. These will be the holes you use to sew on the button.

3 Then add extra holes around the rest of the button. These will be the holes you stitch through, so decide what kind of stitching patterns you will create with them.

4 Allow the clay to dry, following the manufacturer's instructions. Paint the buttons in contrasting colors—remember the sides of the buttons too. Allow to dry.

5 Stitch decorative patterns on the buttons using the stranded floss in contrasting colors. I have used a variety of straight stitches, backstitch, and cross stitch (see pages 8 and 92).

peruvian thread EARRINGS

Create fun and lightweight earrings using jewelry wire and thread. Try layering the thread colors to make different tones and shades.

★ ★ ☆

You will need

- Metal jewelry wire
- US size ²/₃ (3 mm) knitting needle
- Wire cutters or old scissors
- Earring findings
- Sewing thread in light green, pale pink, magenta
- Scissors

1 Leaving a fairly long end, wrap the jewelry wire tightly around the knitting needle, until you have a coiled piece 4 in. (10 cm) long.

2 Leaving a 6-in. (15-cm) end at the finish, cut the wire. Thread the finishing end into the start of the coil, right around, and out at the end again to curve the coil round, being careful not to squash it. Cross the two wire ends at the top.

3 Join the ends by twisting them together, then thread on an earring finding. Bend the twisted end over and twist onto itself to secure in place.

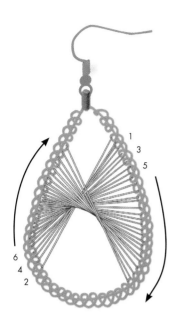

4 Tie the light green thread onto the wire inside the coil, near the top of the earring, and wrap it around the spiral diagonally as indicated. Each wrap should go into the next groove of the spiral.

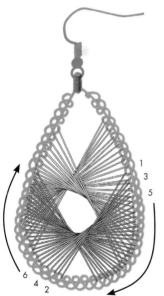

5 Repeat with the pale pink thread, joining it toward the bottom of the green wraps, and wrap as shown.

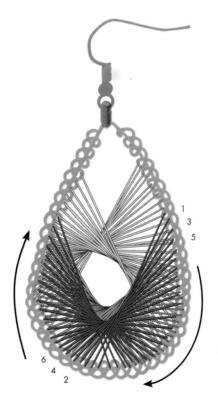

6 Finally add the magenta thread toward the bottom of the earring and wrap as shown.

7 Thread the loose threads into the spiral to neaten. Repeat the steps to make the second earring.

bird BROOCHES

So tweet! Cute wooden bird brooches with simple stitched details—
these will look lovely pinned to a jacket or purse.

★ ★ ★

You will need

- **Wooden bird shapes, about 2 in. (5 cm) wide**
- **White acrylic paint**
- **Paintbrush**
- **Drill with ⅟₁₆-in. (2-mm) drill bit**
- **Needle**
- **Scissors**
- **Embroidery floss in turquoise, coral, lilac,**
- **Brooch pins**
- **Glue gun**

1 Paint the front and sides of your wooden birds with white acrylic paint and allow to dry.

2 Drill small holes through one of the birds in the shape of a chest patch.

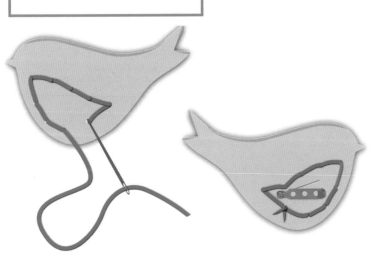

3 Using turquoise embroidery floss, backstitch (see page 8) through the holes to create the chest patch shape.

4 Turn the bird over and glue a brooch pin to the back.

5 Repeat on the other two birds: one design has a coral wing created in the same way as the chest patch using backstitch, and the other has coral, lilac, and turquoise straight stitches (see page 8) worked at different angles.

Tip

The basic wooden bird shape can be used facing either way, so change things around a bit for more interest.

circles NECKLACE

Create disks of cardstock and decorate them with contrasting threads, then mount on a felt backing and add a silver chain for a really stylish necklace.

1 Cut out two large circles (with a diameter of 1½ in./4 cm) and four small circles (with a diameter of 1 in./2.5 cm) from each of your pieces of patterned cardstock. You will have 36 circles in total.

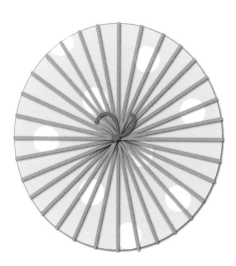

2 Cut 32 small notches evenly around the circumference of the large circles and 16 small notches evenly around the circumference of the small ones. Each notch should be approximately ¹/₁₆ in. (1–2 mm) deep.

3 Choose a thread in a contrasting color to one of the card circles and wind it around each pair of notches from one side to the other. Tie the loose threads in a tight knot on the back and trim.

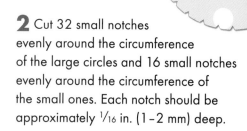

4 Repeat on all the remaining circles. Arrange the disks on your felt piece to make a pleasing pattern. Place some on top and some under each other to create a layered effect.

5 Use the glue gun to stick the circles to the felt. Allow to dry, then trim around the edge so you cannot see any of the felt. Cut the chain into two equal lengths.

6 Make a small hole at the top of the piece on either side and attach a jump ring (see page 11) to each. Thread one piece of chain through each of the rings.

7 Join the two loose ends of each chain together using another jump ring. Attach a lobster claw clasp to one of the ends to complete.

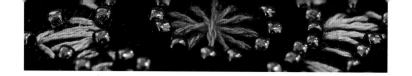

day of the dead SHOPPER

Stitch and decorate a handy shopper with a colorful skull. "Dia de los Muertos" is a Mexican festival to commemorate and remember those who have passed away, and skulls are a popular symbol for the day.

You will need

- **28 x 20 in. (70 x 50 cm) piece of black wool fabric**
- **Tape measure**
- **Scissors**
- **12 x 10 in. (30 x 25 cm) of fusible interfacing**
- **Iron**
- **¼ oz (10 g) metallic black seed beads and beading needle**
- **Sewing needle**
- **Black and pink sewing thread**
- **Tracing paper**
- **Pencil**
- **Embroidery floss in yellow, pink, purple, orange, blue, lime**
- **Sewing machine**
- **28 x 20 in. (70 x 35 cm) piece of pink wool fabric**

1 Cut two strips measuring 28 x 2 ⅜ in. (70 x 6 cm) from the black fabric for the handles. Cut another piece 28 x 20 in. (70 x 35 cm) and cut out a 4 x 2¼ in. (10 x 5.5 cm) rectangle from either side halfway down.

2 Iron the large rectangle of fusible interfacing to the back of one half of the bag. Trace the skull design template on page 117 onto the interfacing—each dot will be a bead.

3 Use black thread to sew a bead on the right side of the bag, over the position of each dot on the wrong side.

20 in. (35 cm)

28 in. (70 cm)

4 x 2¼ in. (10 x 5.5 cm)

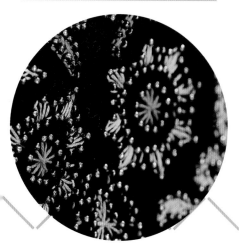

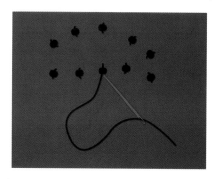

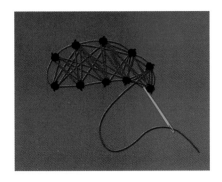

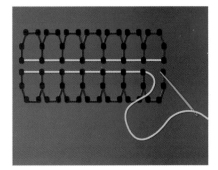

4 Using the template as a guide, fill in the sections with embroidery floss. Solid sections are made up by stitching from bead to bead around the edge to create an outline, and then random stitching between beads inside the shape.

5 To stitch the eyes, work straight stitches (see page 8) between the beads around the outside as shown, using lime floss. The inner circle is made by working straight stitches in orange thread from bead to bead, crossing at the center each time.

6 Make the mouth by working straight stitches between the beads in purple and then green thread. Complete the rest of the sections using the photograph and template as a guide.

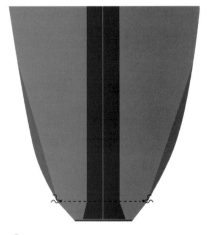

7 To make the handles fold one of the 28 x 2⅜-in. (70 x 6-cm) strips in half lengthwise and press, then open out and fold the raw edges in toward the foldline by about ⅜ in. (9 mm). Fold in half again and topstitch along both long sides. Repeat to make a second handle.

8 Fold the main black fabric piece with right sides together and sew along the side seams to ¼ in. (5 mm) above the cutout rectangle, leaving a ¼-in. (5-mm) seam allowance. Press the seams open.

9 To create the base, fold the bag so one of the side seams runs down the center and the cutout rectangle flattens into a straight seam across the corner. Stitch the seam, then repeat on the other side. Turn the bag right side out. Fold the top edge to the wrong side by about ⅝ in. (1.5 cm) all around.

10 Cut the rectangles from the sides of the pink fabric as in step 1. Repeat steps 8 and 9 to make up the lining, this time with a ⅜ in. (9 mm) seam allowance, but don't turn it right side out. Place the lining over the black bag with right sides together.

11 Take a handle and insert it into the bag, with the loop of the handle between the inner and outer layers and each end protruding slightly about 4 in. (10 cm) from the side seams. Repeat on the other side with the remaining handle.

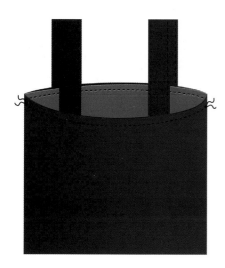

12 Sew around the top edge, leaving a gap 4 in. (10 cm) long unstitched. Turn the bag inside out through the gap. Finish the bag by topstitching ⅛ in. (3 mm) from the edge all around the top to neaten.

NEON necklace

Make a really cool neon necklace from intricate string art circles. If you don't have a macramé board you can use a piece of cork or a pin board.

★ ★ ★

You will need

- 2 pieces of cardstock
- Pair of compasses
- Scissors
- Macramé board
- Pins
- Neon sewing thread in orange, green, pink, yellow
- Craft glue
- Paintbrush
- Jump rings
- Pliers
- 2 pieces of chain, each 12 in. (30 cm) long
- Lobster claw clasp

1 For the orange and green design, cut a 1½-in. (4-cm) diameter circle from the cardstock, place on the macramé board, and place 32 pins around the circumference. Remove the card.

2 Take the orange thread and wrap it around the pins in the order shown. Repeat so that there are two threads on each line making up the star.

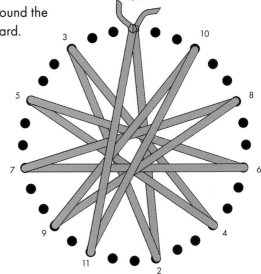

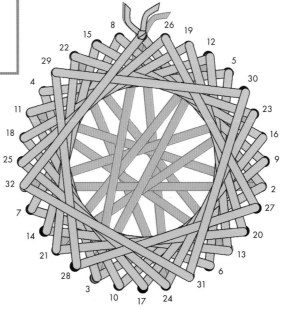

3 Using the green thread, wrap around the pins in the order shown.

4 Soak the threads in watered-down craft glue and allow to dry fully before removing the thread shape from the macramé board.

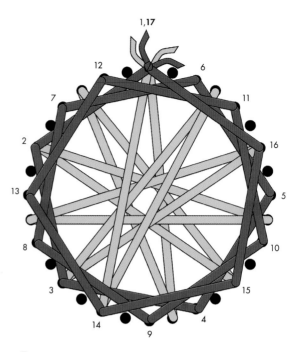

5 For the pink and yellow design, repeat step 1, then work step 2 using pink thread. Finally, use yellow thread to work the top shape in the order shown in the illustration. Repeat step 4 to finish.

6 For the pink and green design, repeat step 1, then work step 2 using green thread. Use pink thread to make the top circle, working in the order shown. Repeat step 4 to finish.

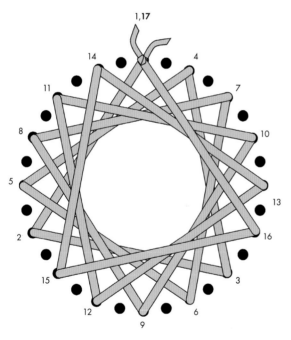

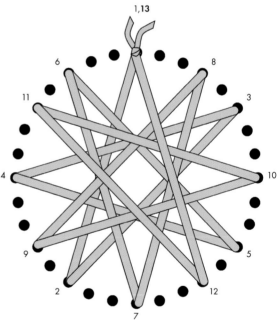

7 For the yellow design, cut a 2⅜-in. (6-cm) diameter circle from the cardstock, place on the macramé board, and place 32 pins around the circumference. Remove the card. Use the yellow thread to create the design shown in the illustration, following the numbering, then repeat the sequence three more times to create a sturdier structure with three threads on each line. Repeat step 4 to finish.

8 For the green design, cut a 2¾-in. (7-cm) diameter circle from the cardstock, place on the macramé board, and place 32 pins around the circumference. Remove the card. Use the green thread to create the design shown in the illustration, following the numbering, then repeat the sequence three more times to create a sturdier structure with three threads on each line. Repeat step 4 to finish.

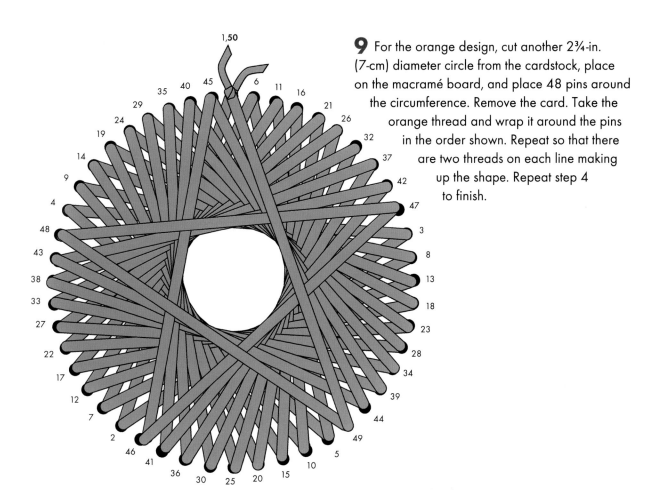

9 For the orange design, cut another 2¾-in. (7-cm) diameter circle from the cardstock, place on the macramé board, and place 48 pins around the circumference. Remove the card. Take the orange thread and wrap it around the pins in the order shown. Repeat so that there are two threads on each line making up the shape. Repeat step 4 to finish.

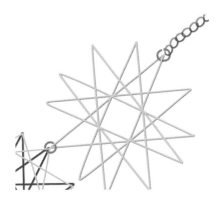

10 Place the circles in a pleasing arrangement and attach them together at convenient points using jump rings. Attach a length of chain at each end of the panel of circles using jump rings (see page 11). Add a lobster claw clasp to the end of one of the chains, and a jump ring for it to fasten to at the other.

pineapple PURSE

Pineapple motifs are so on-trend right now, and you can follow the crowd with this tropical purse! Perfect for holidays and sunny days, this bag is a real summer favorite of mine.

You will need

- **20 x 56 in. (50 x 140 cm) piece of mustard linen fabric**
- Scissors
- **20 in. (50 cm) length of green linen fabric**
- **20 in. (50 cm) length of netting fabric**
- **12 in. (30-cm) square of fusible interfacing**
- Sewing machine
- **Sewing thread in green, dark green, mustard**
- Sewing needle
- **Embroidery thread in dark green, lime green**
- **20 square stud brads**
- **10 in. (25 cm) yellow zipper**
- Iron

1 Cut a strap 2³⁄₈ x 56 in. (6 x 140 cm) from the mustard linen. Then use the templates on pages 118–119 to cut out one bag gusset, two zipper sides and two bag panels in each of the mustard linen, green linen, netting, and fusible interfacing. Cut 14 leaves in green linen.

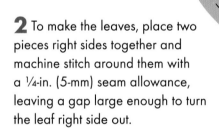

2 To make the leaves, place two pieces right sides together and machine stitch around them with a ¼-in. (5-mm) seam allowance, leaving a gap large enough to turn the leaf right side out.

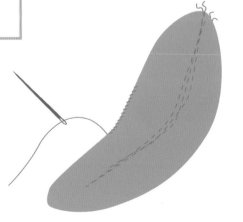

3 Turn the leaf right side out and close the gap with invisible hand stitches. Sew a central stem in dark green thread using straight stitch on the sewing machine. Repeat steps 2 and 3 to make six more leaves.

4 Layer up the outer bag pieces by ironing the fusible interfacing to the wrong side of the mustard linen gusset, zipper sides, and bag panel. Layer the net on the right side of each piece and baste in place. Take one of the bag panels and draw a diagonal grid on the wrong side.

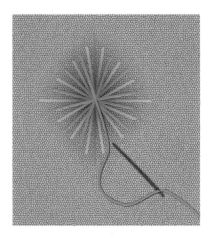

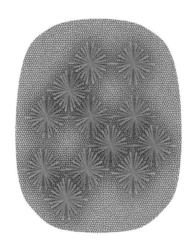

5 Using lime green and dark green embroidery, use straight stitches (see page 8) to sew a diamond on the right side of the bag piece within one of the diamonds of the grid, with the stitches radiating from a central point.

6 Repeat on random diamonds on the panel to create a pineapple texture, using the photograph as a guide.

7 Place studs in some corners of the diamonds, by pushing the prongs of the brad through the fabric and opening them out on the wrong side.

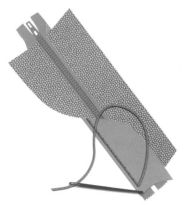

8 On the zipper sides, iron one long edge of each piece of fabric to the wrong side overlapping by ³⁄₈ in. (1 cm). Open out the fold on one piece and place it right side down on the zipper, with the fold close to the zipper teeth. Sew along the fold line, then fold the fabric back away from the zipper. Repeat with the other zipper fabric on the other side, so the zipper has a strip of fabric on each side with the stitches hidden.

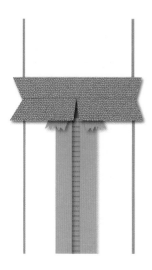

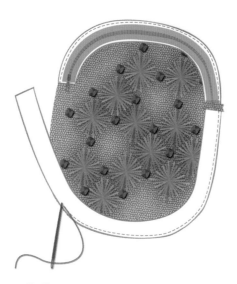

9 Place one end of the zipper section right sides together to a short end of the gusset and stitch in place with a ¼-in. (5-mm) seam allowance. Press the seam open.

10 With right sides together and ensuring that the zipper section is positioned in the center of the top edge, sew the gusset to the front bag panel.

11 Where the gusset meets the other end of the zipper section, stitch them together to create a complete circle. Sew the back bag panel onto the other side of the gusset and zipper piece.

12 Fold the strap in half lengthwise and press, then open out and fold the raw edges in toward the foldline by about ⅜ in. (9 mm). Fold in half again and machine stitch along both long sides.

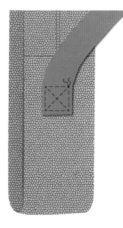

13 Turn the short ends inside the strap and sew the ends to the sides of the bag in a square shape with a cross in the centre.

14 Arrange the leaves you made in steps 2 and 3 at the top of the front of the bag, layering them by following the photographs as a guide, and stitch to the pineapple using green thread.

15 On the green zipper sides, iron one long edge of each piece of fabric to the wrong side by ⅜ in. (1 cm) as before. With the folded edges slightly apart, stitch these pieces to one short end of the green gusset with a ¼-in. (5-mm) seam allowance. Press the seam open. Repeat steps 10 and 11 with the green linen, but without the zipper so that there is a slot along the top of the bag lining.

16 Turn the bag outer right side out, but leave the lining wrong side out. Place the lining inside the outer mustard bag and sew the edges of the slot to the underneath of the zipper so that all raw edges are hidden.

chapter three

ARTFUL
GIFTS

stitched NOTEBOOKS

Add some personality to simple notepads with these stitched designs.
Either create a "canvas" on which to sew a chevron design
or draw a picture with the threads, as in the dandelion design.

You will need

- A6 and A5 notebook
- Pencil
- Tracing paper
- Drill with $\frac{1}{32}$-in. (1-mm) drill bit
- Needle
- Scissors
- Stranded floss in cream, brown, lime green
- A5 notebook
- Ruler
- Stranded floss in turquoise, dusky pink, yellow, maroon, lilac, lime green

Dandelion

1 Trace the template on page 119 onto the front of the A6 notebook.

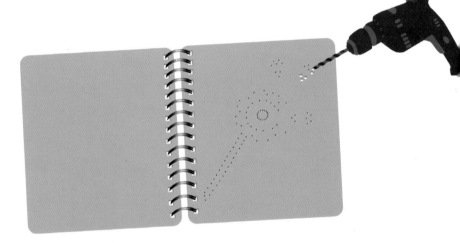

2 Use the drill to make holes through the front cover at all the marked points.

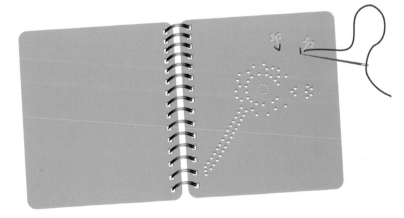

3 Divide the cream, brown, and lime green stranded floss into two threads each and sew the design, using the photograph as a guide.

Chevrons

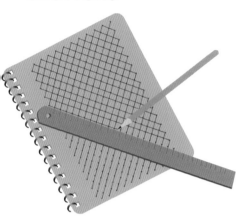

1 With the ruler and pencil, draw a diagonal grid on the front of the A5 notebook. Each diamond should have sides measuring approximately ³/₈ in. (8 mm).

2 Drill a hole through the front cover at each point where the lines cross.

3 Using the stranded floss in turquoise, dusky pink, yellow, maroon, lilac, and lime green, sew vertical and horizontal straight stitches and backstitches (see page 8) to create a chevron pattern. Follow the design given, or develop your own pattern.

yarn-covered LETTERS

Ideal for weddings, a child's bedroom, or just around the home, yarn-wrapped letters are a great way to use up scraps and personalize your space. Why not add a hook to the back of the letter, so that it can be hung on a wall?

★ ★ ★

You will need

- Yarn scraps in dark gray, light gray, pink, lime
- Scissors
- 10¼-in. (26-cm) high papier mâché letters
- Glue gun
- 12 x 10 in. (30 x 25 cm) piece of gray felt for each letter
- Pen

1 Start by cutting some short—about 4 in. (10 cm)—lengths of the yarn that you want to cover the ends of the letters. I used dark gray for the top, bottom, and inside of the curve, and light gray for the underside of the stroke and the end of the curve.

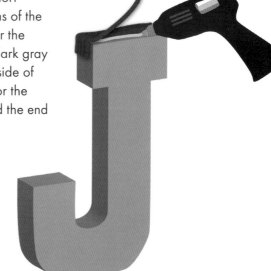

2 Working one yarn at a time, apply a thin strip of glue and lay a piece of yarn on top of the letter.

3 Repeat until the whole surface is covered.

4 Do the same on the bottom, inside the curve, under the stroke, and on the end of the curve.

5 Now wrap the main part of the letter. Apply dots of glue at the start and end of each color to hold the yarn in place.

6 Once the letter is fully covered, draw around it onto the felt, then cut out the felt shape slightly inside the line so it is smaller than the letter. Apply to the back of the letter using the glue gun, to hide all the messy ends.

embroidered vintage POSTCARDS

Enjoy searching your local thrift stores and vintage markets for old postcards,
then update them with geometric patterns stitched in fluorescent colors.
Pop them in simple frames for a fabulous gift or wall display.

★★★

You will need

- Vintage postcards
- Ruler
- Scissors
- Tracing paper
- Pencil
- Pin
- Sewing thread in neon orange, green, pink
- Sewing needle
- White frames

Diamond design

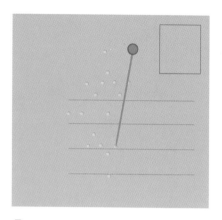

1 Using the illustrations above as a guide, mark the holes for onto the back of your postcard. Use a pin or needle to pierce each hole.

2 Double the neon orange thread and sew the design as shown, using backstitch (see page 8).

Square design

Using the photo to the left as a guide, pierce the pattern on the next postcard, and use neon green thread to stitch this design in backstitch.

Circle design

1 Using the illustration to the right as a guide, draw a circle about 3 in (7.5 cm) in diameter and make 70 evenly spaced holes around the circumference. The holes will be numbered from 1 to 35 on each half of the circle.

2 To work the first curve, take the neon pink thread and make a stitch between 2 and 3. Then make a stitch between 3 and 5, and then another between 4 and 7. Keep repeating this sequence so that each stitch increases by one hole and gets increasingly longer to create a lovely curve.

3 Repeat until the last stitch is between the two holes numbered 1.

4 Then begin again with the second number 1 hole on the other half of the circle, working between 1 and 2, then 2 and 4, then 3 and 6 and so on, finishing at 31 to 27 so that there are two curves opposite each other.

wrapped glitter GARLAND

Use your string to wrap card templates, then layer them up and string them together to create a pretty garland. This would look lovely in a child's bedroom or an office.

You will need

- Glitter cardstock in silver, gold, green, blue, pink
- Pencil
- Scissors
- Cotton thread in gray, mustard, pink, blue, green
- Large pin
- Split pins
- 80 in. (200 cm) string

1 Using the templates on page 120, cut out one of each shape from each color of cardstock.

2 Take one of the flower centers and wrap a contrasting color thread around alternate spokes approximately five times. Repeat on the other set of spokes, using another contrasting color thread.

3 On a large bulbous flower in a different color cardstock, wrap a contrasting color thread around alternate spokes about 25 times. Then take a similar color thread to the cardstock and wrap around the other alternate spokes. Repeat the sequence. Press down to flatten the flower petals.

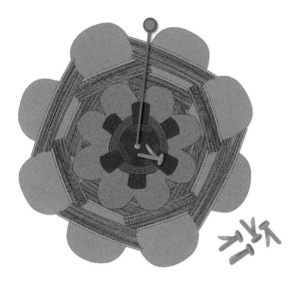

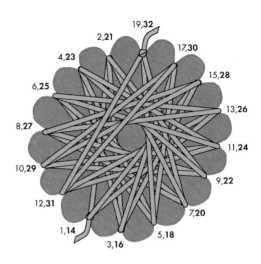

4 Layer up the large flower with a different color bumpy middle-sized flower and the flower center wrapped in step 2. Make a small hole through the center of each with a pin and connect them with a split pin.

5 For the second flower, take a middle piece and wrap in the sequence shown using a contrasting thread.

6 On a large flower (B) in different color cardstock, wrap alternate spokes using two contrasting thread colors. Layer up with the piece made in step 5 and a three-spoked center piece (F) in a third color. Make a hole as before and connect the pieces with a split pin.

7 Repeat with the other shapes to make ten flowers, five of each shape. Arrange so the flower shapes are alternated and attach to the string by knotting it to the back of each split pin.

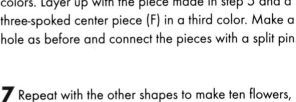

cross stitch fruit COASTERS

Brighten up a friend's table by giving them some fruity cork coasters. Use a simple cross stitch to create the pattern. Almost good enough to eat!

You will need

- 4 round cork coasters
- Ruler
- Pencil
- Needle
- Scissors
- Embroidery floss in purple, cream, yellow, orange, teal, coral, jade, black, light yellow, green, brown

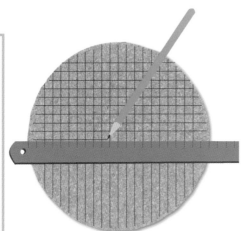

1 Draw a square grid 18 rows by 18 rows, centered on the back of each coaster.

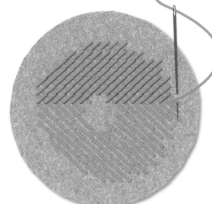

2 Follow the templates on pages 121–122 to sew your designs, working a cross within each square of the grid. Work all the diagonal stitches in one direction first, and then go back to complete the cross by working in the opposite direction.

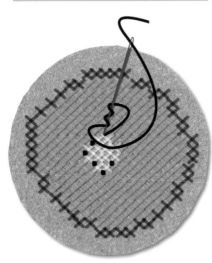

3 On the kiwi design, work French knots (see page 11) in brown around the center for the seeds.

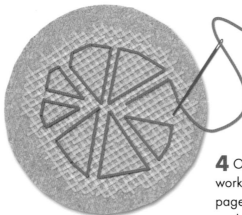

4 On the orange design, work long straight stitches (see page 8) in orange to create each triangular segment.

stitched GREETING CARDS

Add an extra-special personal touch to greeting cards by stitching into them and creating texture. These retro designs are perfect for celebrating birthdays or new homes, for giving thanks, and for showing your love.

1 Scan and print one of the designs on pages 122–123 onto each sheet of cardstock, ensuring the design is on the right side and centered on the right-hand half of the sheet.

You will need

- Scanner and printer
- 11½ x 8¼ in. (29 x 21 cm) sheets of cardstock
- C5 envelopes
- Stranded cotton floss in turquoise, yellow, pink, orange, olive green, lime green
- Needle
- Scissors

2 Fold each card in half so the design is on the front. Using one, two, or three strands of floss depending on the effect you require, begin stitching into your cards.

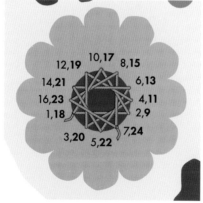

3 On the small five-petal flowers, sew small straight stitches (see page 8) in a contrasting color thread to create a V on each petal radiating from the center. Make a single long straight stitch on each petal of the large daisy-petal flowers, using a contrasting thread.

4 The inners of the large solid-color flowers are created by following the stitching order indicated, using a contrasting color thread.

5 Finally sew across the mini hearts using matching thread and long straight stitches.

Heart design

Outline the shape with running stitches (see page 8) using olive thread.

House design

Use the turquoise thread to sew around the triangular roof tiles. Sew around the edge of the windows using lime backstitch (see page 8). Create windowpanes with orange thread. Outline the door window frames with olive green.

Jug design

Work around the triangles on the jug with the olive green, pink, and turquoise threads. Finally work on the flowers, as for the heart.

Cake design

Work running stitch in pink and yellow around the plate. Backstitch around the frosting and the candle in turquoise. Finally work on the flowers, as for the heart.

Tip

For a neat finish, you could cover the stitching on the inside by gluing a sheet of paper over it.

arrow PILLOW

This arrow-themed pillow will add a touch of style to any couch. The design is stitched rather than wrapped, but this gives a similar effect.

★★★

You will need

- **52 x 20 in. (130 x 50 cm) piece of striped burgundy wool fabric**
- Water-soluble fabric pen
- 135 pearl beads
- 120 bronze beads
- Sewing needle
- Sewing thread
- Scissors
- Embroidery floss in burgundy, teal, aqua, mustard
- Sewing machine
- 16 x 16 in. (40 x 40 cm) pillow pad

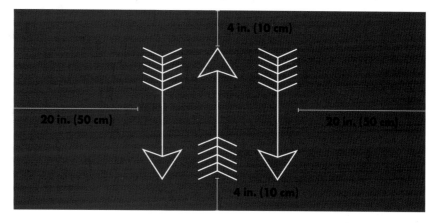

1 Using the template on page 124, mark out where the arrows will go on your fabric and draw them onto the fabric using the water-soluble pen.

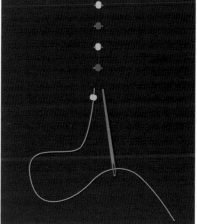

2 Using the sewing thread, stitch a bead every ³⁄₈ in. (1 cm) along each line of every arrow, alternating pearls with bronze beads.

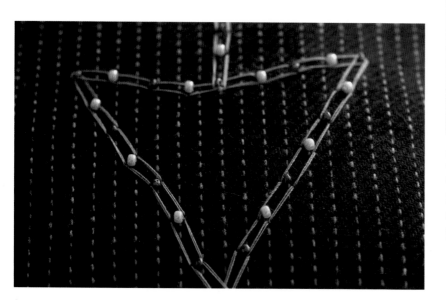

3 Switch to the embroidery floss to make a double line of parallel straight stitches (see page 8) with the beads in the middle, to give the string-craft-wrapped look. Make the first stitches down the line of beads on alternate sides, stitching from bead to bead and going through the fabric under the bead to swap sides. Then work back the other way to fill in the gaps, using the same stitching holes so that the stitches butt up to one another. The heads of the arrows are worked in mustard thread, the shaft in teal, and the feathers of the tail in aqua.

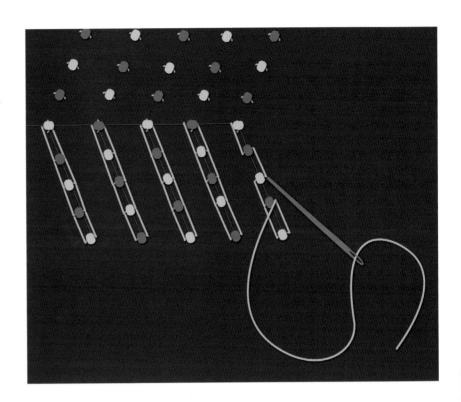

4 Hem both short ends of the fabric by folding the ends under twice to the wrong side, and sewing with the burgundy thread on the sewing machine.

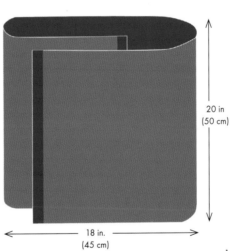

18 in. (45 cm)

20 in (50 cm)

5 Then, with the right side facing inward, fold the fabric to make an envelope that measures 18 x 20 in. (45 x 50 cm).

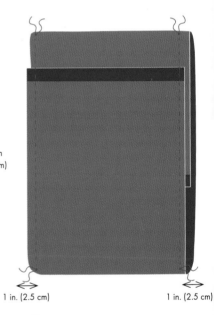

1 in. (2.5 cm)   1 in. (2.5 cm)

6 Sew down the two open edges with a 1-in. (2.5-cm) seam allowance. Turn the cover inside out and insert the cushion pad.

string-wrapped BOTTLE

Make funky string-wrapped vases from old bottles. This is a great way to add some color to your table display—perfect for a party or wedding.

You will need

- **Glass bottle**
- **Yarn in red, cream, gray**
- **Glue gun**
- **Scissors**
- **Yarn needle**

1 Starting from the bottom and working upward, wrap yarn around the outside of the bottle. Use a dab of glue just at the beginning and end of each color to secure.

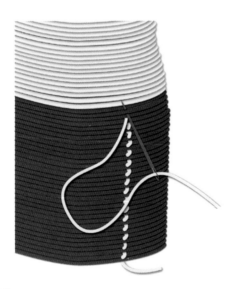

2 Once the bottle is completely covered, cut a length of yarn and weave it through the "weft" of your bottle.

3 Repeat around sections of the bottle, alternating the thread colors you weave through, to create woven stripes up the bottle.

4 Glue the bottom ends of the woven threads to the underside of the bottle, and trim away any at the top to neaten.

ceramic HEART DECORATIONS

Whether these are used as Valentine's gifts or just as decoration around the home, they are pretty and show off your clever stitching!

You will need

- Oven-bake clay
- Rolling pin
- Heart cookie cutter, small round cutter
- Toothpick
- Fork
- Embroidery floss in aqua, jade green, dark green, burnt orange, peach, pale pink, mid pink, dark pink
- Needle
- 10-in. (25-cm) lengths of ribbon in aqua, peach gingham, pink stripe

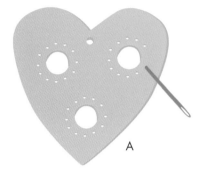

A

1 Roll out the clay to a thickness of ¼ in. (5 mm) and cut out three heart shapes. Add a hole for the ribbon near the top of each heart. Use the round cutter to cut out three holes from hearts A and C and only the bottom hole from heart B. Use the toothpick to make 12 holes equally spaced around each large hole in heart A.

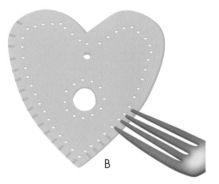

B

2 Use the toothpick to make 12 holes equally spaced around the large hole in heart B, and 46 equally spaced holes all around the edge. Add texture around the edge using the prongs of a fork.

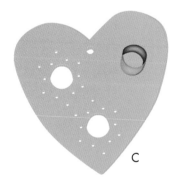

C

3 On heart C, make 16 holes around each large hole arranged in a star shape, as in the illustration. Bake the clay shapes according to the manufacturer's instructions and allow to cool.

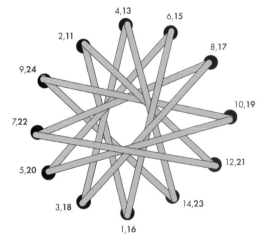

4 On heart A, use the aqua thread to stitch around the top left hole in the order shown. Repeat on the other two holes, using jade green for one and dark green for the other. Thread the aqua ribbon through the ribbon hole and knot at the top to make a hanging loop.

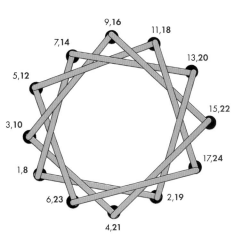

Diagram labels (clockwise from top):
9,16 · 11,18 · 7,14 · 13,20 · 5,12 · 15,22 · 3,10 · 17,24 · 1,8 · 2,19 · 6,23 · 4,21

5 On heart B, stitch around the hole in the order shown using peach. Add stitching around the edge using burnt orange, stitching through each hole twice to make the V shapes. Use the peach gingham ribbon to make a hanging loop as in step 4.

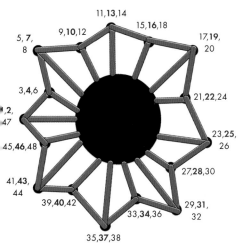

Diagram labels:
11,13,14 · 15,16,18 · 9,10,12 · 17,19,20 · 5,7,8 · 3,4,6 · 21,22,24 · 1,2,47 · 23,25,26 · 45,46,48 · 27,28,30 · 41,43,44 · 29,31,32 · 39,40,42 · 33,34,36 · 35,37,38

6 Finally, on heart C stitch the top left hole in the order shown, using the pale pink thread. Repeat on the other two holes with the mid pink and the dark pink. Make a hanging loop with the pink striped ribbon.

geometric GIFT TAGS

Add a personal touch to your gifts with these geometrically stitched gift tags. Made with cardstock and embroidery floss, they are very quick and easy to create.

You will need

- **Cardstock in turquoise, lilac, green, purple, pale blue/green**
- **Tracing paper**
- **Pencil**
- **Scissors or craft knife**
- **Sewing needle**
- **Embroidery floss in purple, jade green, lilac, blue, coral**
- **Hole punch**
- **10 in. (25 cm) of cord in green, blue, pink**

1 Using the templates on page 126, trace the designs onto the cardstock and cut out. Score along the central dotted line. Mark up the stitching hole positions from each template.

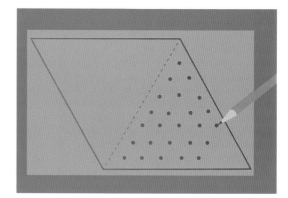

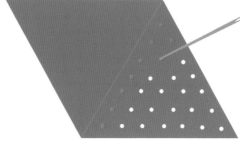

2 Make the holes in one half of each shape, using a needle.

Triangle design

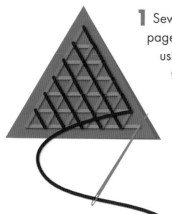

1 Sew the design in backstitch (see page 8) as shown in the illustration, using purple, then jade green, then lilac floss—each color is stitched in straight lines but parallel to a different edge of the triangle.

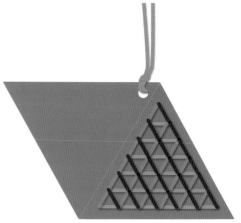

2 Make a hole in the back of the gift tag using the hole punch. Fold a 5-in. (12.5-cm) length of green cord in half and thread the loop through the hole, then pull the ends through the loop.

Circle design

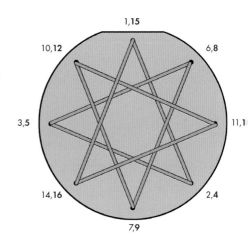

1 Using blue floss, sew the design by knotting the floss end and bringing the needle up through to the front at 1. Then stitch in the number order on the illustration—every other stitch will be on the reverse of the cardstock.

2 Add a hanging loop as for the triangle, using the other half of the green cord.

Hexagon design

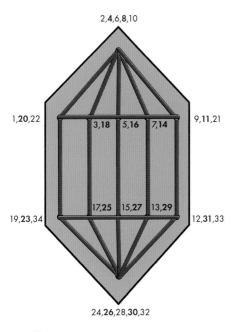

1 Using coral floss, sew the design as in step 1 of the Circle.

2 Add a hanging loop as for the Triangle, using half of the blue cord.

Octagon design

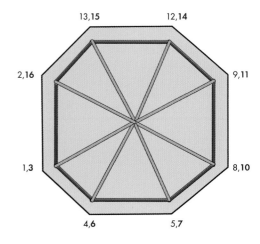

1 Using purple floss, sew the outer design as in step 1 of the Circle. Then use jade green floss to stitch from the center hole to each point of the octagon in turn.

2 Add a hanging loop as for the Triangle, using the other half of the blue cord.

Pentagon design

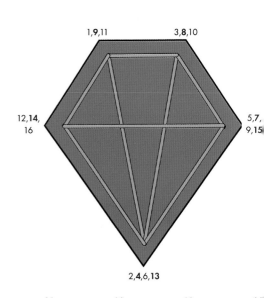

1 Using lilac floss, sew the design as in step 1 of the Circle.

2 Add a hanging loop as for the Triangle, using half the pink cord.

stitched GIFT BOXES

Gorgeous little boxes, ideal for packing small gifts or simply for keeping your own valuables safe. I have used plain papier mâché boxes, but colored boxes would look even more stunning!

Heart box

You will need

- Heart-shaped, square, and round gift boxes
- Pencil
- Sewing needle
- Embroidery thread in red, green, turquoise, purple, light green

1 Draw a heart in the center of the top of the lid. Pierce 18 holes evenly around the heart outline, using the needle. Pierce 36 holes around the sides of the lid near the top edge, spacing them out evenly.

2 Using the red thread doubled, knot the end on the inside of the lid. Sew random stitches from the heart-shape holes in the top to the holes around the edge until you can clearly see the shape of the blank heart in the center. Keep stitching until you are happy with the effect.

Square box

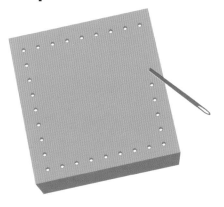

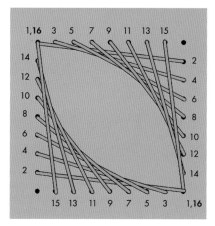

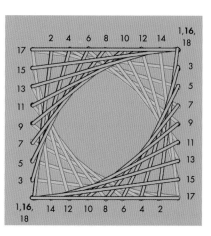

1 Draw a square on the lid just inside the edge. Use the needle to make a hole in each corner of the square, and then make seven evenly spaced holes on each side.

2 Using the green thread doubled, knot the ends on the inside of the lid. Stitch each half in the order shown.

3 Then use the turquoise thread, doubled in the same way, to stitch each half of the second layer in the order shown.

Round box

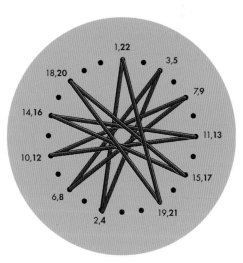

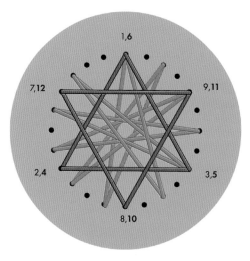

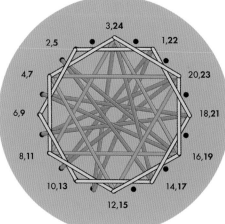

1 Draw a circle on the lid that is slightly smaller than the top, and make 24 holes evenly spaced around the circumference. Using purple thread doubled, knot the ends on the inside of the lid and stitch the design in the order shown.

2 Now take the red thread and sew a star in the order shown.

3 Use the light green thread to stitch the final layer in the order shown.

4 To finish, work backstitch (see page 8) around the edge of the circle using turquoise thread.

wooden KEY RINGS

Show off your stringing skills with these mini wood star key rings. Colorful threads are stitched through holes in the wood to create different effects.

★ ★ ☆

You will need

- Tracing paper
- Pencil
- 3 wooden disks, each approx. 2³⁄₈ in. (6 cm) diameter
- Clamp
- Drill with ¹⁄₁₆-in. (1.75-mm) drill bit
- ¹⁄₈-in. (3-mm) drill bit
- Sewing needle
- Stranded embroidery floss in purple, orange, turquoise, teal
- Scissors
- 3 split rings

1 Using the templates on page 125, draw one design on each wooden disk. Make the holes using the smaller drill bit, plus one hole using the larger drill bit near the top edge of each disk.

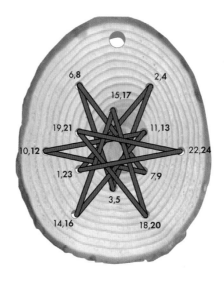

2 To make the purple star, use all six strands of the purple floss. Knot the end on the back behind hole 1, then follow the stitching order shown.

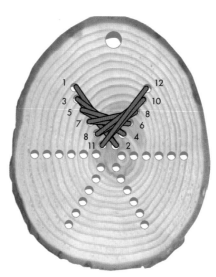

3 To make the multi-colored star, use two strands of each color floss. First use the orange, knotting the ends on the back and following the stitching order shown. Repeat on the next section in the same order, using turquoise and then in the next using purple. Repeat in the same color sequence in the next three sections to finish the star.

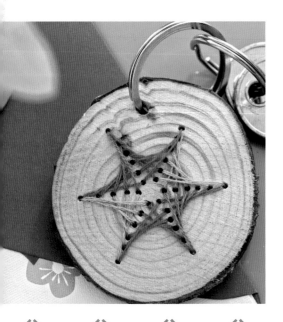

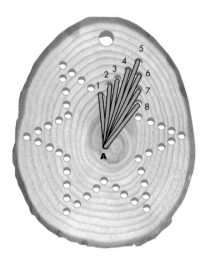

4 For the final design, take one strand of the turquoise floss and, knotting on the back and starting from center hole A, work outward around the star in the order shown, going back to A each time. Once each section of the star is filled, work backstitch (see page 8) around the edge in teal.

5 Thread a split ring through the hole at the top of each wooden disk to complete.

Tip
Hold the wooden disks firmly in a clamp so they don't move as you drill them.

Templates

Most templates in the following pages are printed at full size, so can be used at the size they appear. Some are printed at half size, which means they need to be enlarged by 200% or 400% using a photocopier before you can use them. For some projects, you may need to transfer a template using tracing paper. To do this, place a sheet of tracing paper over the template and secure with masking tape. Trace the lines or dots with a hard 4 (2H) pencil, then turn the tracing paper over and go over the design again on the reverse with a soft 2 (HB) pencil. Now turn the tracing paper over again and place it in position on your chosen object. Go over the design carefully with the 4 (2H) pencil, then remove the tracing paper. This will give you a nice clear outline.

STRING ART OWL page 16

Enlarge by 200%

DRIFTWOOD FEATHER page 14

Actual size

GEOMETRIC STITCHED LAMPSHADE
page 20

Enlarge by 400%

STRING DREAMCATCHER page 36

Actual size

FLOWERS IN A JAR page 39

Actual size

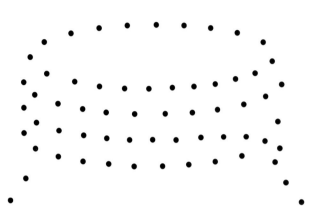

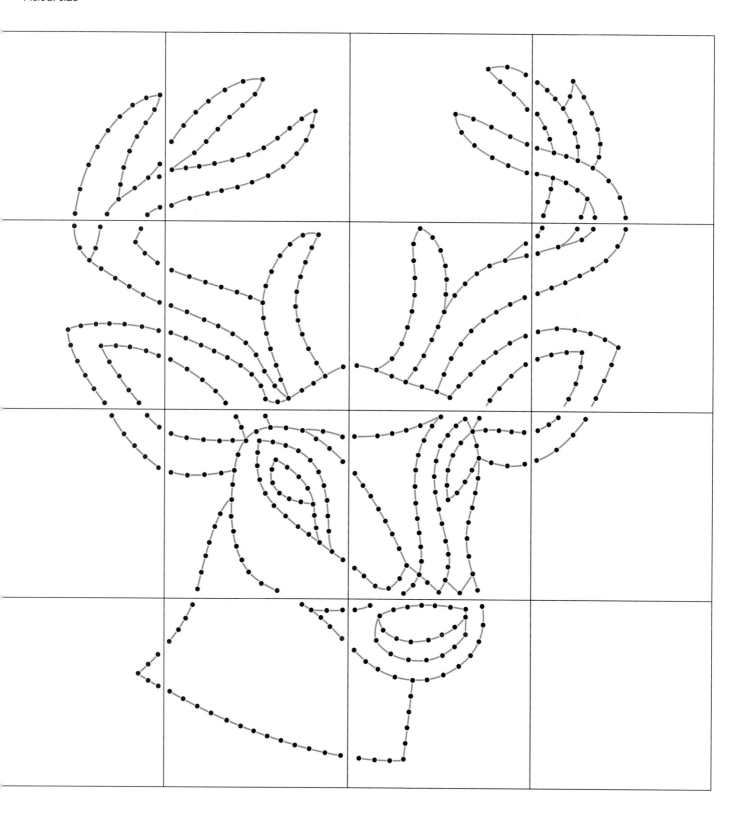

Part of placemat, enlarge by 200%

Coaster and part of placemat, actual size

Coaster, actual size

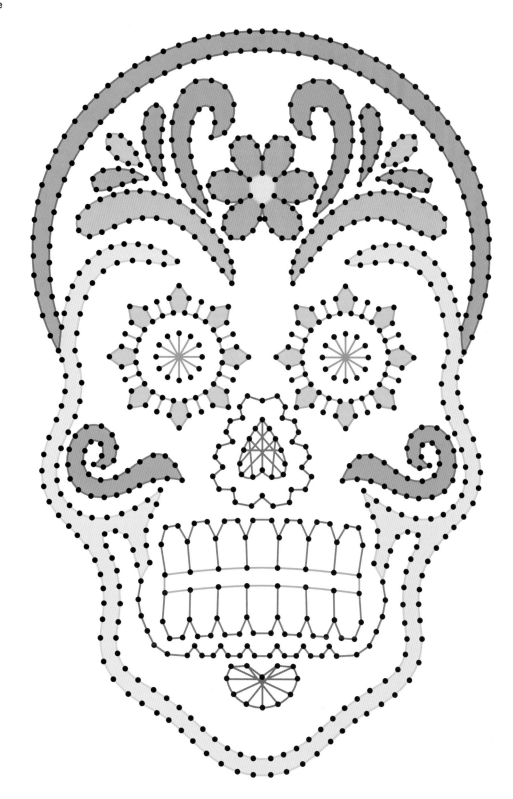

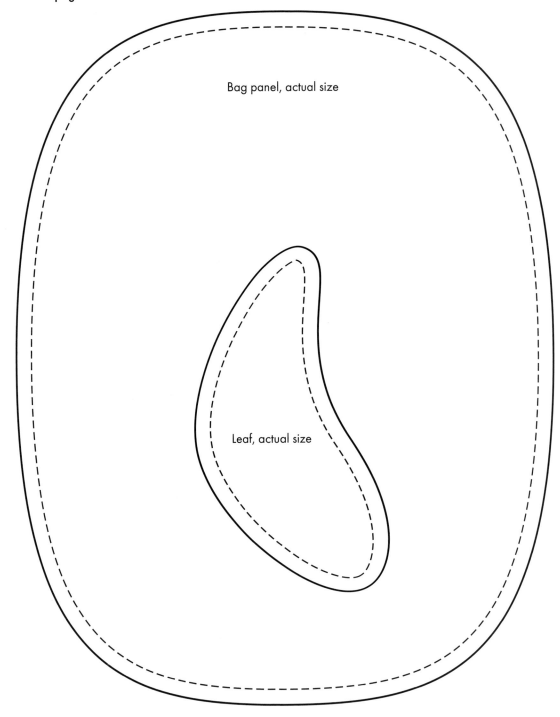

Bag panel, actual size

Leaf, actual size

Zipper side, actual size

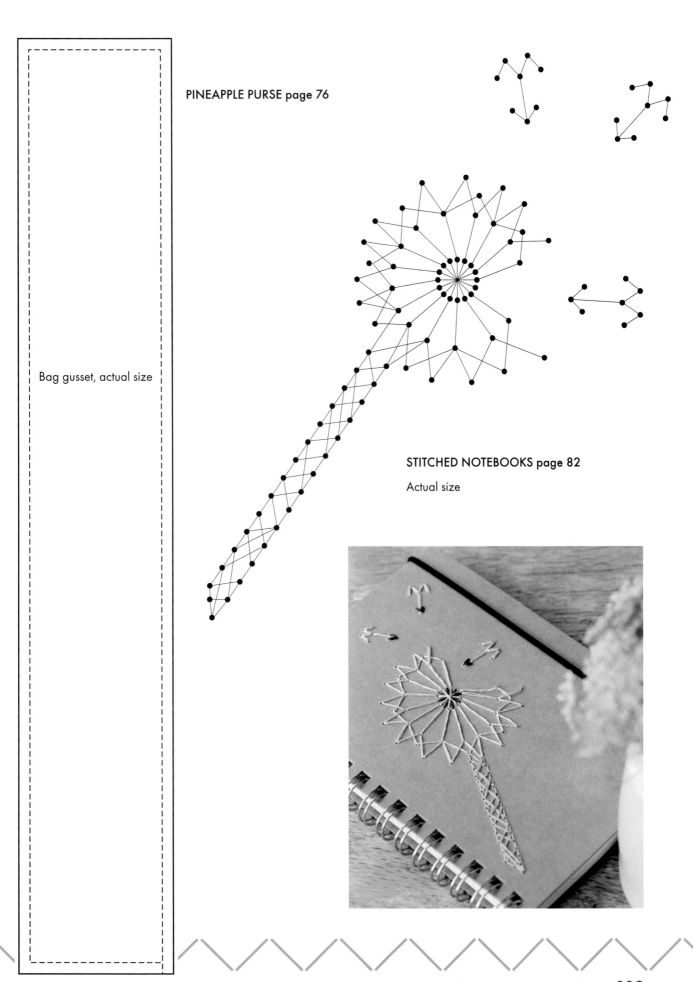

PINEAPPLE PURSE page 76

Bag gusset, actual size

STITCHED NOTEBOOKS page 82

Actual size

WRAPPED GLITTER GARLAND page 89

Actual size

CROSS STITCH FRUIT COASTERS page 92

Actual size

CROSS STITCH FRUIT COASTERS page 92

Actual size

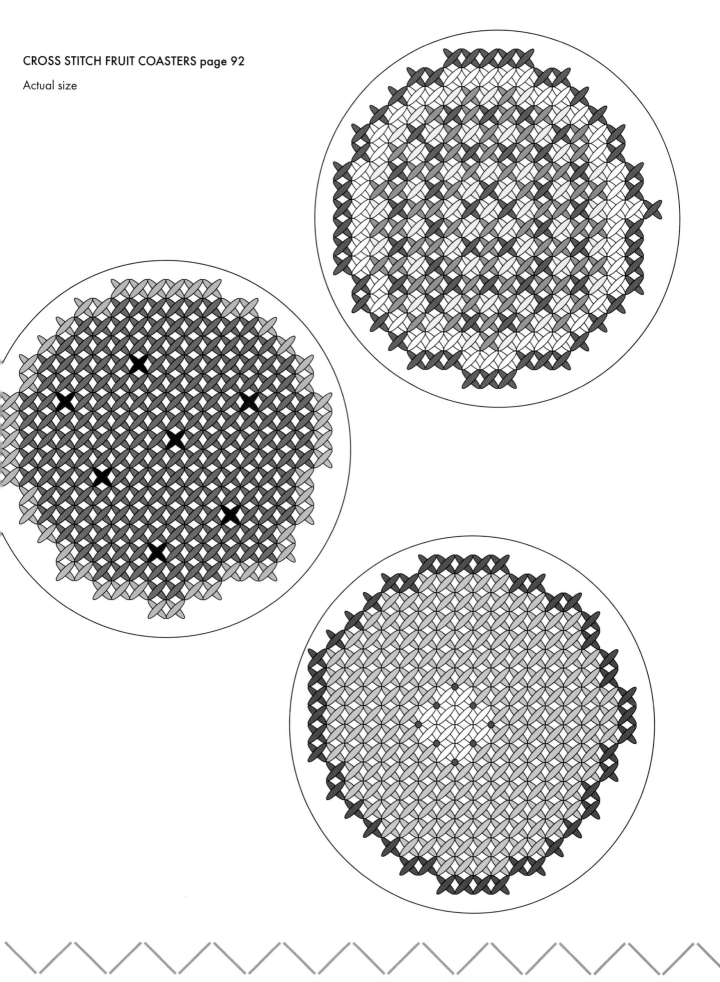

ARROW PILLOW page 97

Enlarge by 200%

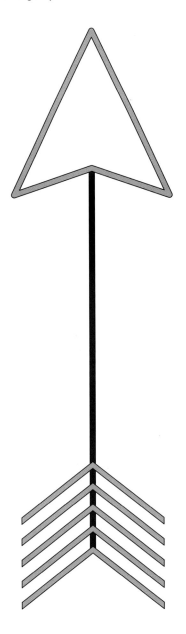

CERAMIC HEART DECORATIONS page 102

Actual size

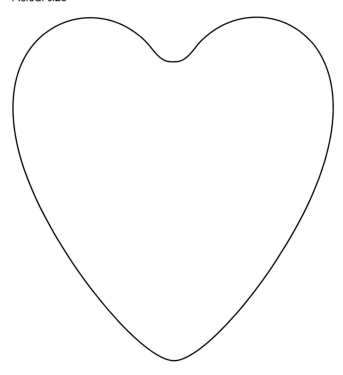

WOODEN KEY RINGS page 110

Actual size

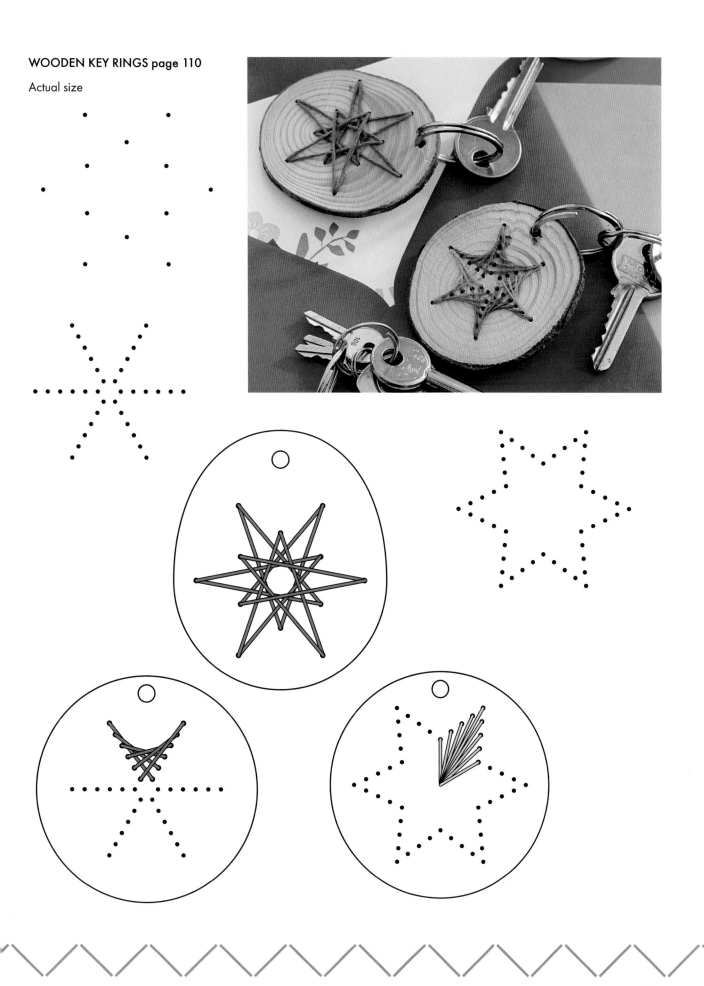

Enlarge by 200%

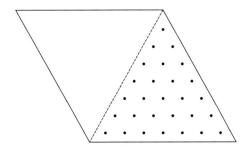

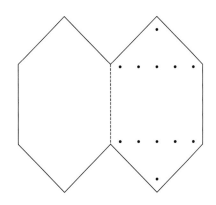

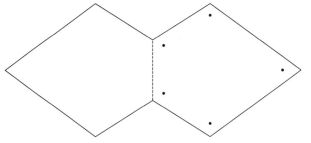

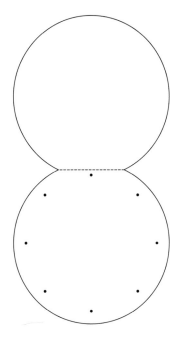

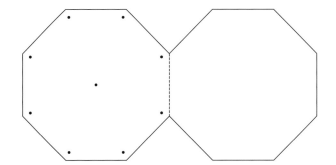

Suppliers

NORTH AMERICA

A.C. Moore
www.acmoore.com

Ace Hardware
www.acehardware.com

Britex Fabrics
www.britexfabrics.com

Buyfabrics
www.buyfabrics.com

Fabricland
www.fabricland.com

Hobby Lobby
www.hobbylobby.com

Jo-Ann Fabric and Craft Store
www.joann.com

Michaels
www.michaels.com

Purl Soho
www.purlsoho.com

UK

Abakhan Fabrics Hobby Home
www.abakhan.co.uk

Crafty Crocodiles
www.craftycrocodiles.co.uk

Hobbycraft
www.hobbycraft.co.uk

Homebase
www.homebase.co.uk

Ikea
www.ikea.com

John Lewis
www.johnlewis.com

Muji
www.muji.eu

My Fabrics
www.myfabrics.co.uk

Wilko
www.wilko.com

ACKNOWLEDGMENTS

Huge thanks to everyone at CICO; the book looks wonderful, as CICO titles always do. Gorgeous styling and photography, great illustrations, and excellent editing have all come together brilliantly. Thank you to all who have worked on *String Craft*, especially Marie, Louise, and Anna who I worked with on almost a daily basis.

Thank you, of course, to my husband and extended family for all the support they give to make the writing of these books possible, especially with an on-the-move one-year-old! I wouldn't be able to manage it without you.

Index